Pennsylvania's Adams County Ghosts

**FEATURING
GETTYSBURG,
NEW OXFORD,
CASHTOWN,
& VICINITY**

Steve McNaughton

Schiffer Publishing Ltd

4880 Lower Valley Road, Atglen, Pennsylvania 19310

Other Schiffer Books on Related Subjects:

Ghosts of Valley Forge and Phoenixville,
978-0-7643-2633-2, $14.95

Firestorm at Gettysburg: Civilian Voices June-November 1863, 0-7643-0618-9,$39.95

Pittsburgh Ghosts: Steel City Supernatural,
978-0-7643-2891-6, $12.95

Type set in Bard/NewsGoth BT
Designed by Stephanie Daugherty

ISBN: 978-0-7643-3123-7

Printed in China

Schiffer Books are available at special discounts for bulk purchases for sales promotions or premiums. Special editions, including personalized covers, corporate imprints, and excerpts can be created in large quantities for special needs. For more information contact the publisher:

Published by Schiffer Publishing Ltd.
4880 Lower Valley Road
Atglen, PA 19310
Phone: (610) 593-1777
Fax: (610) 593-2002
E-mail: Info@schifferbooks.com

For the largest selection of fine reference books on this and related subjects, please visit our web site at:
www.schifferbooks.com
We are always looking for people to write books on new and related subjects. If you have an idea for a book please contact us at the above address.

This book may be purchased from the publisher. Include $5.00 for shipping.Please try your bookstore first.You may write for a free catalog.

In Europe, Schiffer books are distributed by
Bushwood Books
6 Marksbury Ave.
Kew Gardens
Surrey TW9 4JF England
Phone: 44 (0) 20 8392-8585
Fax: 44 (0) 20 8392-9876
E-mail: info@bushwoodbooks.co.uk
Website: www.bushwoodbooks.co.uk
Free postage in the U.K., Europe; air mail at cost.

Dedication

M y one and only love for my entire adult life, my wife Tina, has stayed by my side providing the support and encouragement that I so knowingly needed to get through the process of writing this book. Even though there were days, even weeks or months when she was ready to clobber me for going off in my tangents, she stuck in there and never let me give up. For all that she has given to me and for all that she will never realize, how can I ever repay her? I guess all I can say is: Tina, thank you and I love you now as I did when we first met and always will, even beyond our time in these bodies and on this plane of existence.

3

Acknowledgements

With great thanks and respect, I need to acknowledge my sister-in law, Debra Walke who provided her insight and guidance in preparing me for writing this book. And then there is Allen Gross from Roanoke Virginia (ghosthunter1863@yahoo.com), who came into my life during this process and has boosted my knowledge of paranormal investigating. Allen's expertise in investigating and specifically in spirit photography has been invaluable to me and has created what I hope is a lifelong business relationship and, most importantly, friendship.

I also need to acknowledge Allyson Walsh and her twin sister Adele Nichols; together they're known as the psy-dentical twins. I got to know Allyson and Adele through some of our bed and breakfast guests and they have proven their psychic abilities many times by helping us determine who is walking with us as a spirit in Adams County. If it were not for Allyson and Adele, we would have never been able to take their psychic impressions to the Adams County Historical Society and track down the families and histories of the spirits that co-exist with us in New Oxford and Chestnut Hall.

I also want to thank everyone who opened their homes and businesses, allowing me to record their stories and encounters as well as allowing P.E.E.R. to conduct investigations. Not only to satisfy their own need for answers, but to help with my own curiosity of the paranormal and of course the creation of this book. And lastly, I want to thank all the members of P.E.E.R. for their contributions and efforts in our paranormal investigations. Thanks Brandy and Bob Dockey, Jan and Steve Bolze, Elaine Gerwig, Stan Wannop, Mik and Marty Wheeler, Jim and Joseph Zero, and Vivian and Allen Gross. Thanks to all of you and let's keep it together.

Contents

Introduction:

Reasons for a Haunting

D id you ever wonder what makes a place haunted? Have you asked why there are ghosts or spirits here in this place? Do they really exist or is it just my imagination? Is my deceased father still around and can he see and hear me, or are we alone in this world? Are we ever really alone? Well, I would like to provide a possible answer to some of these questions for you. I don't know if I can completely convince all or any of the harshest skeptics and pure non-believers out there, but in my attempt to search out the answers for myself, I've become more and more of a believer and a less of a skeptic.

Yes, I am a skeptic. I think most of us have said at one time, "I'll believe it when I see it." I was one of those people, and yes, I've *SEEN* it with my own two eyes. These personal experiences is what keeps me questioning, snooping, researching, and investigating. It is our own skepticism that makes us a better investigator. The one most important thing that I need to do in order to answer these questions as a skeptical paranormal investigator, and that I encourage you to do as well, is 'keep an open mind.' Skepticism alone is not enough. With skepticism alone, you are sure to never believe or trust anything regardless of an outcome. Skepticism must be balanced with openness and the ability to listen, truly listen, and put in place what makes sense after the investigation and research fails to provide the obvious, the normal, and the natural.

Let me suggest some possible answers for you by starting with the first question; what is it that makes a place haunted? First, it is important to realize that it just might not be the place that is haunted. A person or a possession such as a favorite chair can be haunted, and that haunted person or possession can remain haunted as he, she, or it moves around from one house to another, one town or part of the world to another. It is this belief that on occasion gives me pause and almost always makes me question, "Are we ever really alone?" Have you experienced this phenomenon yourself? Have you ever thought that you are being watched as you go about your normal life and work? I have. Let me tell you about one of my many personal experiences. It began in the spring of 1993 a few months after my father's death. He and my older brother had a swimming pool service business and had several contracts to open some area pools after their winter shut down. With my dad gone, I volunteered to help my brother with these existing contracts. One afternoon we had just removed the cover from a large in-ground pool and spread it out on the lawn so I could scrub it down and get it ready for storage until it was needed again in the autumn. It was a very warm and sunny day, and I wasn't in the mood to hurry as I hosed and scrubbed the vinyl liner. It was then that I heard my brother say, "Hurry up; we need to move it before it burns the grass." "Okay," I said. As I spun around to reply, oddly enough, my brother was nowhere near me. He was at least one hundred feet away on the other side of the pool on the other side of the property. Then it hit me. I realized that the voice I heard was not my brother's; it was my father who had just spoken to me. And at that same moment, I got a whiff of smoke like that from the extinguished cigarettes that I had smelled so often as a kid growing up. Dad had smoked as long as I can remember even though in his later years he had curtailed his smoking to a minimum. I haven't had the opportunity to hear from my father since that day, but many times, perhaps dozens of times since that day, I have gotten a whiff of that same smoke, and I know then that my father is there. I have smelled that smoke in my previous home, at work, in my car, and in my new home in New Oxford. My wife has even smelled it a few times when we were together. With that realization, I'm content. I know that he is still here, watching my family and me as we continue our lives until the day that we can again exist on the same plane. I have concluded that it is easier for them to see and hear us than it is for us to see and hear them. Man, I wish I could change that.

So here you see that it is not the place that is haunted... it's the person, in this case, *ME*. Now follow me on these next set of experiences as I throw a little twist into the mix. I live in a 120-year-old Victorian house in New Oxford just a few miles east of Gettysburg. I have had my share of paranormal experiences in and around this house, proving to me that it has its fair share of spirits hanging around. I have counted at least six different and distinct spirits in this house. I have determined that most of them belonged to the same family who lived most if not all of their lives in this house. I have heard a voice from one of them, I have seen with my own eyes a spark of light slowly flash on the wall right in front of me, and I have seen an orb of light the size of a grapefruit poke its way through a door only to retreat into the closet. (I guess it didn't like what it saw.) I have washed away fingerprints from the stainless steel refrigerator, and I have been poked in the back and had my shirttail tugged. Are these hauntings of a person or the property? In my opinion, these are hauntings of the property. Even though they are intelligent and may interact with me, they are doing so because they are grounded to this house. I am in their home, where they continue to exist. But I don't want to get ahead of myself; I'll save these stories for when we get to the chapters covering New Oxford.

I have also found that inanimate objects can be haunted as well. Perhaps a person had a favorite car and centered much of their life on that car, pampering it and paying attention to its mechanical idiosyncrasies, details, and polishing its fine lines. Then one day when the owner dies, the car never runs again. Or maybe it is a bedroom vanity mirror that on occasion shows the reflection of the woman who peered into it each morning and evening. These would be perfect examples of haunted objects and possessions, a residual haunting. One such instance of a haunted object will be revealed in an antique mall in the chapter covering New Oxford.

Now that I have explained how a haunting can be tied to a person or thing as well as a place, let's get back to that first question; what is it that makes a place haunted? Most everyone I've spoken with who has experienced a haunting firsthand indicated that they sensed *intelligence* associated with the haunting. If intelligence is present, then there either is or at one time had to be a life associated with whatever it is that they experienced. This does not mean that all intelligence was once human. There are natural spirits as well, but that is for another book. For all intents and purposes, in the reference of this book, the intelligence of that life is the spirit or energy of a once living person.

Why Adams County?

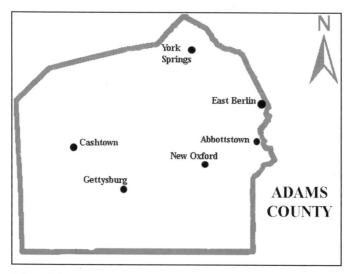

York
Springs

East Berlin

Cashtown

Abbottstown

New Oxford

Gettysburg

N

ADAMS COUNTY

A few of the haunted towns in Adams County.

But why is it so concentrated in Adams County? Because in the heart of Adams County is a little town called Gettysburg and over a three day period in July 1863, more than 50,000 people died within approximately a seven-mile radius from the heart of that town. In comparison, that is nearly seven times the current day population for the town of Gettysburg according to the 2000 census. With that much death, as brutal and as quick as it was, the energy of many of those people still roam the fields, streets, and buildings in and around Gettysburg and throughout the surrounding towns in the county.

But there is more to Adams County than Gettysburg. Adams County in South Central Pennsylvania was founded in 1800 when the western section of York County was mapped out and separated, forming the new county that was named after John Adams, our country's second President. The 2000 census indicated that Adams County's population was just over 91,000 and the 522 square mile area of land is mostly rural with Gettysburg, the county seat, centrally located. Gettysburg is surrounded on three sides by the Gettysburg National Military Park and it is this large section of land that gives Gettysbury its fame to claim...the site of the Battle of Gettysburg. The Gettysburg National Military Park has become the focal point of Adams County and a large draw of tourists from around the world.

As written in Wikipedia, the county's "mid-19th century roadway pattern remains intact today. Thirteen historic roadways converge at or near Gettysburg Borough. Two circular rings of towns surround Gettysburg; the first ring is typically found at a distance of about seven miles from Gettysburg. The second ring is found at a distance of twelve to fifteen miles from the County Seat." In these two rings of towns, I have visited homes and talked with families and friends who have experienced paranormal events, documenting their stories here so they can be shared with you.

We will visit the towns of Gettysburg, New Oxford, Cashtown, and several other small towns throughout Adams County. However, before I take you for a stroll through Adams County, I would like to provide a few definitions of some of the terms used in paranormal investigations and describe the purpose of the equipment I used during these investigations. If you are already familiar with the terminology and equipment used in paranormal investigating, you may wish to jump to the next chapter but hey, it's only a few pages, humor me and read on.

Paranormal Terminology

EVP (electronic voice phenomena): During interviews, vigils, and investigations, I used an audio recorder or a camcorder. Sometimes, when recordings are played back, voices that were not heard during the real time conversation are present. Sometimes these voices are clear and distinguishable while other times they can barely be made out. Sometimes it's not a voice, but a noise such as footsteps, doors opening and closing, tapping, or knocking. The key distinction or determining factor is that the persons present during the recording did not hear these voices or noises in real time. They're only discernable or heard on the tape or electronic recording. If the voice or noise was not heard while recording, then it's known as an EVP or electronic voice phenomenon.

EMF (electromagnetic field): Spirits use energy to make things happen. It might be to move around themselves, make other things move, or even make themselves manifest as an orb, ectoplasm, or as a visible being. It is also speculated that they have some energy of their own, but many times will zap the energy from a nearby source such as a battery, or directly from the atmosphere causing a sudden drop in air temperature. When this energy (known as an electromagnetic field) is concentrated into one location, it can be detected with the appropriate equipment, an EMF Detector.

Vigil: On occasion, investigations lend themselves to a period of time when persons will gather to sit, in an attempt to communicate with spirits that may be in that area. This has nothing to do with a religious ceremony or the use of an Ouija Board. During a vigil, many prefer to take the time to be still and quiet, only to ask questions in hopes of having a communication with a spirit. Tape recorders, thermal scanners, camcorders, and EMF detectors will be used to gather, verify, and validate any anomalies.

Ghost Hunt: A ghost hunt is performed at a location where there has been no previous evidence of a haunting. This is sometimes a more casual event utilizing less staff and equipment.

Ghost Investigation: A ghost investigation is performed when there have been reports of a haunting that has already taken place. The investigation is approached with a plan of action to answer the what, where, when, who, and how questions.

Residual Haunting: This type of haunting can best be thought of as if a person were watching a video or movie. An object or a place can capture the energy of an event and when atmospheric conditions allow, the event will be played back over and over as if recorded in time. Keep in mind that a piece of tape used in audio and video recordings is just film to which the images and sounds can adhere. One cannot interact with residual hauntings; one can only see or hear them as they repeat themselves, trapped in time. How many times have you heard a door close or someone walk up or down the stairs or hallway? That just might be a residual haunting.

Intelligent Haunting: The intelligent haunting is just that. One might see a partial or full-bodied apparition. Someone might answer a question or move an object upon request or one just might experience a bump in the night. A person may smell an odor such as smoke when there is none to be found. One may see an orb, a cloud of ectoplasmic mist, but most commonly, a shadow will pass in a person's peripheral vision. These spirits are grounded or earthbound, continuing to exist or live in this plane. Most persons believe that these spirits have yet to 'see the light and cross over.' I believe that this is not necessarily the case; a spirit can go about in this world wherever it chooses and, many times, it does not choose to leave his or her home.

While we are on the subject of intelligent spirits, I'll offer this point of view concerning their age and appearance: I do not believe in things like a headless horseman or a woman with the head of a goat that walks the streets. I do believe that a person's spirit can walk the earth and interact with us. I also believe that what we see (if we see them) is what they want to project or how they want to be seen and how they see themselves. Consider this: if I were to walk out into the middle of the street and be run over by a truck, I would imagine I would be pretty torn and mangled. I'm dead. Now it is time for me to come back because I don't want to leave my lovely wife. I want to comfort her and continue to offer my advice, thoughts, and my love. Do you think that I would see myself as a mangled mutilated corpse or as I saw myself in life? How do you think I would want my wife to see me? I definitely would not want to scare her. My spirit did not get beat up, only my body. Even though my spirit used this body, the spirit continues, and the easiest way for my wife to recognize me (if she were able to see me) is for me to project the image she remembers. In the same context, the timeline of a spirit's existence is different from that of the body. The spirit may act and appear to be older or even younger than the body it inhabited when it died. I have found this to be the case with one of the spirits in my own house that I believe is that of Reed Flaherty. He is that of a playful child of maybe four or five years, even though in real life, he was but an infant when he died.

Ectoplasm (ecto for short): One dictionary describes ectoplasm as "the substance believed by spiritualists to expel from a medium who is communicating with spirits." Ectoplasm is best described as a cloud or mist. I have seen these clouds with my naked eyes as they crossed my path in my own home, and I have seen it captured on film, twice over my own shoulders. I do not claim to communicate with spirits, but I know they have been there. My friend and spirit photographer Allen Gross has captured these ectos over my shoulders, and it is his theory that I have two spirits that like to follow me around. What causes the ecto phenomenon? I'm not certain, but I believe that it is the energy of a spirit that is near the stage of manifestation.

Orb: A circle, a sphere, or a round object related to the energy of a spirit that is often captured on film. In the paranormal field, it is an object captured on film or seen with the naked eye. Many if not most paranormal skeptics do not believe that an orb is related to the energy of a spirit. They believe that all orbs are nothing more than an error or flaw in the camera's ability to properly focus or is a piece of dust, pollen, or moisture that is floating in the air and too close to the camera lens. Although I will agree that some cameras do have this problem, I do not agree that all orbs captured on film are dust, pollen, or moisture just as I do not believe that everything that falls from the sky is always rain and can be nothing else.

Infrared: The invisible portion of light that makes it possible to see in the dark. Infrared lighting is what is used by video cameras and camcorders to allow recording in a building in the dark or outside at night when it is impractical to use spot or floodlights.

Equipment

I am not a rich man and I do not invest heavily in the field of paranormal investigation. I research to find what equipment is needed to get the job done, and then I research to find a reasonably priced piece of equipment that meets the requirements to do that job. Here is a quick list of the major pieces of that equipment. I do not run cables and cords, I do not tape cameras and lights to the doors or walls, and I do not use onsite-monitoring stations. I don't like to be invasive in someone else's home, and I don't want to be tied down when it comes to a critical moment in an investigation. Keep it simple. After all, the four most important pieces of equipment that a person can use during an investigation is what comes natural to most of us: our ears, eyes, nose, and an open mind with the ability to reason. With that said, here's the hardware list.

Digital Camera: The digital camera is the most commonly used piece of equipment during paranormal investigations. The digital camera does not require the changing, storage, and development of film and can provide quick and immediate verification of an anomaly captured on the disk.

Camcorder: There are several types of video recorders, analog and digital. They use a variety of media tapes and cards or disks and there are other options and accessories to consider. The one accessory that I could not do without however is the additional infrared light, which extends the range of the night vision up to one hundred feet.

EMF Detector: During investigations, I use two types of EMF detectors. The EMF detector I use to take base readings (the property's normal reading) of an area is the GausMaster. Using a needle gauge and an audio signal, it will quickly let you know if there is an electrical anomaly present. In addition to the GausMaster, a KII EMF detector is recommended. This device uses a series of five lights to indicate the presence of electrical discharges and has been said to be of assistance in having communications with spirits through a series of questions that can be answered with a 'yes' or 'no.'

Audio Recorder: The audio recorder is perhaps one of the simplest pieces of equipment to use on an investigation; yet, it can become one of the most important. Not only does it record interviews with property owners, but it can also record sounds that were not heard during the investigation. Countless EVPs (electronic voice phenomena) have been documented as answers to questions during investigations. Many questions are asked in an attempt to establish who the spirit is and why it's present, so don't dismiss the audio recorder. If you buy an analog recorder, be sure to get one with an external microphone so you can eliminate some of the recorder's internal mechanical noises.

Thermal Detector: Like all the other pieces of equipment mentioned in this list, the thermal detector comes in several different styles and has multiple purposes. There are detectors that will read surface temperatures and ones that will read air temperature. The latter is perhaps the most usable and accurate for paranormal investigating since a drop in air temperature can indicate the presence of a spirit.

As with all the equipment listed above, you can spend a little cash at a time and establish a reasonably usable set of equipment, or you can lay out a small fortune and maybe even end up on TV. Perhaps the most important piece of advice that I can offer is learn to use the equipment before showing up at the investigation site. Practice at home, in the backyard and with a neighbor or best friend. It really does not matter how long it takes to learn how to use the equipment and interpret its readings and findings, just do it.

The Farnsworth House Inn

G hosts are not very fussy about where they live. I just know that they do live. I've found them and heard about them in the most remote parts of the county, along the noisiest of highways, on the busiest sidewalks, and in the most popular buildings in downtown Gettysburg...like the Farnsworth House on Baltimore Street. So, where do we begin our journey in Adams County? I guess I could begin anywhere, but for you I'll begin in the southern half of the county, in the most popular town that is known worldwide as a haunted town, Gettysburg, Pennsylvania.

There are scores of books that have been written about the hauntings in Gettysburg and many of them have concentrated on the battlefields surrounding the town. Gettysburg is a town that, if it were not for the bloodiest battle of the Civil War taking place here on July 1, 2, and 3 in 1863, might be as little known as any other small town in the United States. *It is known for the battles and it is known for its ghosts both in and around town.* One drive through the south end of town on nearly any Saturday night and you can see more than one tour group walking the streets of Gettysburg. So where is it in town that I want to take you?

Since we are talking about the streets of Gettysburg in the south end of town, let's begin there with the Farnsworth House Inn at 401 Baltimore Street (www.farnsworthhouseinn.com). Named in memory of Brigadier General Elon John Farnsworth, the original part of the building was erected in 1810, with a brick structure added in 1833. It was occupied by the

Sweney family during the Civil War. Today, the property is operated as a restaurant and an inn.

Looking at the south wall of the Farnsworth House, you will see over 150 pockmarks dotting its surface. At first glance, you will think that these white marks are mere defects. Inches below the roofline on this same wall is a small window in the garret from which Confederate sharpshooters took their aim at Union soldiers on the next ridge as the Battle of Gettysburg raged for three days. In an attempt to curtail the onslaught from the distant Confederate sharpshooters, Union soldiers pocked the side of the house with bullet holes. It is claimed that it was one of the Confederate sharpshooters staked out in the garret that accidentally shot and killed Jennie Wade, the only civilian killed during the three-day battle of Gettysburg. Speculation has it that the sharpshooter was taking aim on the doorknob of a little house in an attempt to confirm his aim and set his sights. The shot did not hit its intended mark, instead it passed straight through the wooden door into the kitchen where Jennie Wade was struck and killed. Today, that line of fire from the Farnsworth House to the Jennie Wade House (www.jennie-wade-house.com) is blocked by a Holiday Inn that was so intrusively plopped amongst the little houses on the south end of town.

Entering the Farnsworth House is like stepping back in time to the mid 1800s. As soon as you enter the main lobby, the décor is as it may have appeared during the Civil War with the few exceptions of modernization to accommodate the dining public and overnight guests. The property has been updated and expanded over the years, but the main house still maintains the aura of what it once was. John McFarland is the man who built the house in 1810 and added the brick portion

The Farnsworth House in Gettysburg. Take note of the bullet holes on the wall.

to the house in 1833. The room named for him is located in that original portion of the house. The McFarland Room offers two brass single beds and is accented with vintage clothing and an antique sewing machine. Named for the 16th President of the United States is the Lincoln Room, which is located off the courtyard and garden area. Dawned with a high four-poster bed, the room is decorated with Victorian cabbage rose wallpaper, an antique prism chandelier, and a black marble gas fireplace. A replica of the rocking chair, which President Lincoln sat in at the time of his assassination at Ford's Theatre, and original newspaper articles of the Lincoln funeral procession, completes this room. Back on the second floor are several other guest rooms. The Catherine Sweney Room is located next to the Sara Black Room and has a queen size bed and some antique furniture. It is named for the family that owned the home at the time of the battle. It's private bath with tiled floor and antique claw foot tub and Victorian high tank pull chain commode keep with the later Victorian period. The Sara Black Room is also named for a previous owner of the house and is located in the brick portion of the main house that was added in 1833. The room has a lace topped canopy bed and an antique marble-top dresser that compliments the room's decor. When gazing out one of the front windows, one wonders who was watching the procession on that infamous day when Abraham Lincoln rode past on his journey to deliver the Gettysburg Address.

So who is it that haunts the Farnsworth House? I'm told that there are over a dozen different spirits there, but most of the stories concern a midwife named Mary and an eight-year-old boy named Jeremy. Mary's story is that she had delivered two babies in the house for the Sweney family; one of those babies was stillborn. Mary was a wonderful midwife and caregiver who had always taken care of the family and all their needs, but when the stillborn baby was in her hands, it was more than she could bear. It is said that even today, Mary takes care of the people, tourists included, staying in the house. Guests will wake up in the morning or return to their room from a day on the town to find their dirty clothes folded and placed in a neat pile or a jacket that was tossed over a cradle in the room, hung on a hook. When staff is approached about this, the tourists are informed that it is not the cleaning staff picking up after them...it is Mary. Some guests have also reported that Mary has been seen at the foot of their bed, wringing her hands, mumbling the words, "It's not my fault, It's not my fault." Distraught over the stillborn baby, Mary has committed herself to caring for the occupants of her master's house. And by the way, there is one more way you can tell if Mary has been in the area. Mary loved roses and many times when she is around, you will be able to smell the fragrance of roses in the air, a lingering perfume that is easily distinguished from the manmade scents of today.

And then there was Jeremy. Jeremy was an eight-year-old boy like any other boy who lived in a small town in 1855. He was full of life and vigor, and he was mischievous and loved to play games. Up until the day he died, one of his favorite games was called 'chicken.' Now chicken was not played back then as it is today. Back then, you played chicken with yourself—it was all about whether you had the nerve and agility to get in personal contact with a team of horses that were running full steam up the street. Here's how the game of chicken was played in 1855 in Gettysburg.

The Farnsworth House, then owned by the Sweney family, is located between two hills on Baltimore Street. Teams of horses were whipped into a full gallop as they pulled wagonloads of supplies from the warehouses at the south end of town, up the hilled street, and into the market area at the town center. Just as the team crested the top of the first hill, they were pushed even harder to gain speed to clear the next hill. To avoid distractions, the horses were outfitted with blinders that eliminated their peripheral vision. As the teams of horses were worked up into a frenzy and gust of speed, Jeremy would run from the sidewalk onto the street and tag the lead horse. Now these horses would not see him coming because they were wearing their blinders, and when they felt a slap on their shoulder, they would often jump or bolt. And this is exactly what happened one day when Jeremy ran out onto the street and slapped the lead horse of a full team.

As he slapped the horse's right shoulder, Jeremy slipped; the horse reared up and brought down his full weight onto Jeremy's chest. Even though this was a game that Jeremy played regularly, this was not how it was supposed to end.

Jeremy's father, who was just up the street watching his son, witnessed him fall and ran to his rescue. As he reached his son, motionless on the dirt street, he felt Jeremy's breath, which was low and weak. He gathered his son in his arms and carried him into the Sweney house where a doctor was called to attend to the broken boy. For hours, the doctor attended to Jeremy as his father paced the hall outside the room, back and forth, smoking his cigar, for what seemed an eternity waiting to see his son. Finally, the door opened and the doctor approached Jeremy's father and informed him that there was nothing more he could do for the boy. He told him that Jeremy's time was limited and that he should go in and say his goodbyes. Rushing into the room, he gently picked Jeremy up into his arms and sat in a chair in the hall. He held onto Jeremy until his breath became faint and then extinct. In preparation for burial, it took three men to coax Jeremy from his father's arms. Many people have reported smelling the smoke from a cigar and hearing the haunting footsteps of Jeremy's father as he paces up and down the hallway. Some have even told of their face-to-face encounter with him in the hallway, just outside the Sarah Black bathroom. Are they witnessing a residual haunting from Jeremy's father? Who is to say? I have not been able to find any documentation of Jeremy's death, his father, or even that they ever existed in Gettysburg. If this is just lore, it is one that has become overwhelmingly strong over the decades. Even people who claim to be skeptics or to have never heard the stories about

Jeremy have provided their own truths as evidence of Jeremy and his father.

Ghost sightings at the Farnsworth House run the gambit from photos with orbs and ectoplasm to seeing someone at the foot of the bed. Before I get into my own experiences at the Farnsworth House, let me share with you a story from my friend Allen Gross. Allen is a leader in the field of ghost investigations and along with his wife Vivian, hail from Roanoke Virginia. Here is his story from a few years earlier:

"Vivian and I stayed in the Shultz Room back in 2005. We met another family there that was staying in the McFarland room. We will call them Jack and Jill and for their daughter who was staying in the Lincoln Room, we'll call her Jane. They invited us into their room to talk about some of the reported hauntings and stories surrounding the Farnsworth House. After probably about an hour of sharing stories, we returned to our room for a rest before dinner. After our nap, as we were heading down the hall to go out for dinner, we heard a scream. Jill came running out her door toward us, grabbed Vivian, and asked if she had just shaken and rattled her doorknob? "No," replied Vivian. "We were up the hallway, nowhere near your door." After dinner, Vivian and I went back up to the TV room when something happened that we could not explain. Around 10 p.m. that evening, the Farnsworth House closed down its dining room facilities and all was quiet in the house. All the staff had gone home for the evening, the doors were locked, the ceiling fans were shut down, and there was no heat or air conditioning needed or being used in the house. We became a little restless and took a walk through the halls toward the Sweney Room where you could either go upstairs to the garret or downstairs to the dining room. As we stood there for a few moments just observing, all of the sudden the door and doorknob to the Sweney Room began to shake vigorously. I thought the door was going to come off its hinges...someone was trying their best to get out of that room. I then looked over to the door of the Sara Black Room, which is adjacent to the Sweney Room. It was not shaking so I knew it was not a vibration going through the house or any type of ventilation system going bad. Whatever this was, it was inside the Sweney Room.

The next morning, Jack and Jill joined us for breakfast. I asked them if they had experienced anything else once we separated after dinner. Jill said that she was very nerved up and took a sleeping pill and her daughter and husband swapped rooms leaving Jack to sleep alone in the Lincoln Room. Jack then began to tell all of us how last night he had been converted from a skeptic to a believer. While he was lying in bed, he felt something get on the bed and touch him. Jumping out of bed in disbelief, he turned the lights on and just stared at the bed. He then became ice cold as he realized that whatever had gotten on the bed was now standing beside him and bumped him as if using their hips to bump him out of the way. The impact from the bump was so strong that it pushed him about two or three feet across the room. When Jack came down to the breakfast table and told this story, a confession of sorts, you could see in his eyes and in his face that a skeptic had turned to a believer. What made his story even more credible is that it was his wife who had made the reservations and he had no prior knowledge that the Farnsworth House was supposed to be haunted.

After breakfast, Vivian asked the cleaning lady if she could see inside the Sweney Room. She needed to see for herself if there were any open windows, any cracks or drafts that could have caused the door to shake so violently the night before. After a thorough inspection of the room, we were convinced that there was nothing in the room that could have caused the door to act the way it did. In fact, the room was in shambles as it was under construction and not being rented out to anyone.

A few years later, Allen and Vivian again traveled to New Oxford, this time to meet up with my wife Tina and

I. Tina and I purchased our home and spent a year and a half renovating and restoring it with plans to open a bed and breakfast. Today, it is known as Chestnut Hall Bed and Breakfast, and is one of the few Queen Anne Victorian style bed and breakfasts in Adams County. Allen and Vivian came north to get together with us so we could visit the Farnsworth House and experience firsthand the Farnsworth's story telling in the 'Mourning Theatre' and the Garret. It was a Monday evening approaching eight o'clock when we met on the sidewalk outside the courtyard. The weather seemed more like the dog days of summer and the temperatures had made an upward swing into the nineties making it the hottest Columbus Day holiday on record. As sunset was at 6:45 that evening, it was clearly dark enough for the crowd that had gathered for the tour to be in the mood of finding ghosts. Through the sounds of the traffic on Baltimore Street, you could hear their cameras clicking and beeping off frame and flash in hopes of capturing an orb or image of a ghostly nature. Well, of course, I was one of them; after all, that's what I do in my spare time. I too wanted to validate over and over again my own belief and search for proof of life on another plane of existence.

The crowd outside the Farnsworth House had grown to over forty people and, as the time approached for the tour to begin, our guides broke us up into two groups; one beginning in the garret (attic) while the other group began in the Mourning Theatre (cellar). We just happened to be in the group that headed up into the garret. As we fished our way through the narrow halls and up several flights of stairs, it became clear that even though the group was now cut down to twenty-three people, we were going to be in

The window in the garret at the Farnsworth House from where the sharpshooters took their aim. Do you see the bullet hole just above the window?

close quarters. As we ascended the last set of steps and crossed the threshold into the garret, we were also reminded by the wave of warm air seeping into the hallway that the summer-like temperature of this October day had spent its time beating down on and penetrating into the confines of this small un-insulated room.

The garret was divided into two sections. The smaller south side was restored and partitioned off; this is where the Confederate sharpshooters took their aim on the Union lines on the other side of the Jennie Wade house. The north side of the garret was lined with two rows of benches for the tourists while the tour guide sat on a chair in front of a few display cabinets housing artifacts and other memorabilia. Our guide for the garret was a young woman, probably in her mid thirties, dressed in period clothing and was both informative and entertaining. Even though her stories provided names and lore including the stories of Mary, Jeremy, and his father, they provided little that I could consider as factual. Most of her presentation was the relaying of tales and stories of both suspecting and unsuspecting guests of the Farnsworth House. I had toured places such as the Shriver House Museum (http://www.shriverhouse.org), which depicts "The Civilian Experience" during the battle. I had hoped for a little more than I received. After about thirty minutes in the garret and hearing the lore of the ghosts at the Farnsworth House and some of the guests' tales, we were permitted to view and photograph the south side of the garret before heading back downstairs and outside to the cellar. It was from this infamous window with such a sorrowful reputation as the portal that provided the opportunity that resulted in the death of an unsuspecting witness to the Battle of Gettysburg, Jennie Wade.

Once we passed the other group of twenty tourists on the sidewalk, we stepped down into the outside entrance to the cellar of the Farnsworth House, which is known today as the Mourning Theatre. Earlier in the day, I had read about this room on their website and had a pre-conceived notion that we were about to experience a re-enactment of a viewing of sorts. I was wrong. There were two coffins in the room, along with period looking clothing, draperies, and rows and rows of chairs. At least it was cool in the cellar. Our young female tour guide from the garret had traded us off on the sidewalk to our new tour guide, a middle-aged man of substantial size and a voice and personality that put everyone at ease and in good spirits. He began his portion of the evening's tour with additional stories and lore, but then proceeded to fill the rest of his time with

The Mourning Theatre in the Farnsworth House—it looks like there may have been someone there other than the living.

more stories of tourists' experiences. Of his stories, the one most interesting to me was of his own personal experience while taking one of his groups to the fields behind the school that was across the street from the Farnsworth House.

He explained to us that to have proof of a ghost was something that he could not provide because one's personal experience was only that unless it was documented and supported with something like a photograph. He told us that it was on one of these tours that his group had just cleared the ridge on the field behind the high school, overlooking the valley, and onto the wooded area at the far end of the field. As he told them a bit of the history of the area and how it was used in the battles, the group had lined up across the ridge, facing him as he had his back to the valley and the woods. He said that the tourists were pointing to a

Confederate re-enactor at the edge of the woods. He turned around, saw the same soldier, and explained to the group his attire and accouterments, commenting on how expertly and authentically he was dressed. At that moment, he noted that the barometric pressure changed, thickening the air, and the soldier turned around and headed off into the woods. As the entire group watched the soldier head off into the woods, the soldier began to lighten and fade with each additional step until he completely disappeared, not into the woods, but into thin air. Not one person had the sense or forethought to snap a single picture. This personal experience, witnessed by scores of people became just that. It is now just another unsubstantiated, unrecorded, un-provable, and undocumented personal experience.

Ending this piece of the Farnsworth tour, our guide displayed and demonstrated the use of divining rods. He explained how each and every thing we do is caused by the electrical impulses from our brains. He eloquently described how each of the highly focused soldiers was intensely concentrating on their role in the battles and how at the moment of their deaths, their energy did not die...it merely became something else (or something like that). His point was that with these divining rods, he could detect that energy and actually communicate with the spirits. He demonstrated this by asking if there was a spirit in the room that wanted to speak with him. Suddenly, the rods crossed as an indication that someone was there. He asked if it was Jeremy and again the rods crossed. In a matter of two or three minutes was what he presented as a brief communication with Jeremy.

After we concluded in the Mourning Theatre, the group headed off for the walking tour. We had had enough and decided to spend an hour in the Sweney Room that Allen and Vivian had reserved for the night. The room was smaller than I expected, but it was appointed very nicely in period style and furnishings. We crouched on the floor around the bed, placed our tape recorder in the center of the bed, and took K2 meters and camera in hand. With the lights turned off, we began asking our questions in an attempt to get someone's attention. It did not matter who showed up—we just wanted someone to make themselves known to us. Again, we were looking for proof. After an hour and over a hundred photos, I called it quits, knowing that I had to get some sleep before getting back up for work in seven hours. After reviewing the photos I had taken in the room, I found nothing—not one single orb, vortex, or puff of ectoplasm. Vivian on the other hand had captured orbs on eight of her photographs. And where were they, you might ask? They were all around my wife Tina. As Allen exclaimed, "I'm telling you, those kids from your place are following you everywhere." The kids that Allen is referring to are Reed Flaherty and Alice Diehl. We'll talk more about them in upcoming chapters about the Chestnut Hall Bed and Breakfast and New Oxford.

Is the Farnsworth House a place you should visit on your ghost hunting expedition of Adams County? Absolutely! Set your expectations where they belong when it comes to taking the tours of the garret and cellar. Realize and understand what they were used for and what roles they played in Gettysburg's history. That in itself will make that portion of the tour worth the few dollars you will pay. Then, spend a few nights in the Sweney, Sara Black, Swartz, Lincoln, or McFarland Room and have your own personal ghostly experience.

Chapter Two:

In the Midst of Battle

Gettysburg & the Surrounding Towns

The Klingel House

The Klingel House near the Peach Orchard and the fields of Pickett's Charge.

Now let's move just outside of town to the fifty-five-acre farm where Joyce Coulter grew up near the fields of Pickett's Charge. It was evident to me that Joyce was proud of her heritage and family. She boasted that her maternal great-grandfather, George Washington Grant Heagey, was the first battlefield guide in Gettysburg. There had been two World Wars involving the United States since the American Civil War by the time Daniel and Margaret Snyder, Joyce's parents, rented and moved into the National Parks Services'-owned farm in April of 1946. Pointing to a wedding photo on the wall, Joyce explained that her parents were married in 1939. They already had two children when they heard that a small farm south of Gettysburg was available for rent. They became the last civilian family to live in one of the Parks Services' houses in Gettysburg. They had two more children and raised their family there, occupying the house for over sixty-one years. The house is a modest farmhouse with the original structure being a log home. Even though the living spaces and the exterior of the house have since been covered, you can still see the exposed logs as you climb to the attic on the steep staircase. Covering the exposed logs became necessary since there were many holes in the chinking due to it taking hits from rifle fire during the Battle of Gettysburg.

Wishing to direct our conversations toward the realm of the paranormal, I asked Daniel if he had ever noticed anything strange or out of the ordinary or if he has ever heard anything ghostly. With a sort of a chuckle and a smile on his face, he replied, "Only a mouse." Now I could have taken that a few different ways and pressed the question, but I decided to leave it alone and consider that he didn't want to add to that discussion for this book.

Joyce then decided it was time to give Tina and I a tour of the house while conveying her stories. We moved from the kitchen, which was located in the rear of the house, to the narrow center room, which was part of the original log house. As long as Joyce could remember, this room had always been used as a sewing room and playroom. There was one single window on the side wall...*a window that had always **haunted** Joyce*. She would see images in the window. As a child and young teenager, she would try to place objects in front of the window to keep the people from looking in. She was never able to make out any faces on the men. She could only see a darkened silhouette of a man's head wearing a hat that, as she describes today, was one worn by soldiers. Even as we stood there in that room, I could sense her uneasiness.

As I listened to Joyce's stories unfold, I soon realized that there might have been a mix of intelligent and residual hauntings taking place in the fields of Pickett's Charge. Could this be residual spirits passing by the window looking for a place to rest or perhaps a hot meal or were they just lost and confused? As we moved to the front room of the house, its age became evident with the large cook fireplace that had since been closed off. During the 1850s when this

The Pennsylvania Monument and the fields of Pickett's Charge.

house was built, this would have been their only source for cooking, heating water, and heating the house. There was one additional fireplace in the house that was in the second floor bedroom directly above this front room.

As a teenager, Joyce and her best friend were inseparable. If Joyce was not at her friend's house, they were together here, in this house on Steinwehr Avenue. As we talked about some of the house's features, Joyce returned to a childhood memory that had reoccurred several times in the house with her friend. There had been several times that a hand would clasp Joyce's shoulder. Startled, she would ask her friend, "Why did you do that? Don't do that." Her friend would always reply in the same way, "I didn't do anything, honest."

Moving up the stairs to the second floor, I had to duck my head as I rounded the corner to keep from hitting the ceiling of the next set of stairs to the attic. Once on the landing of the second floor, Joyce pointed out that the front bedroom was her parents' room, her and her siblings used the center room, and her grandparents used the bedroom to the rear of the house. We walked into the center room and then into the rear bedroom. After her grandparents had passed away, she took over the rear bedroom as her own bedroom. It was a larger room in the house, just over the kitchen, and it still sported the purple wallpaper that she chose as a teenage girl. As a child and teenager using both of these rooms, she felt comfortable most of the time. Being on the second floor and off the ground gave her a better feeling of security. There were occasions when she would hear noises from outside through the bedroom window. They were not the typical farm animal noises that she was accustomed to hearing. She described them as human; not moans or sighs, but not clear words. "It was like mumbling voices, you could tell it was people but you could not actually hear a conversation."

We then walked back to the front of the house to her parent's bedroom. Joyce recalled a time when she was fourteen years old. Her older brother and sister had moved out of the house and her younger brother and father were away at a conference, so Joyce decided to sleep with her mother that night. It was sometime in the middle of the night when Joyce was awakened by a noise coming from the living room below her. As she listened, Joyce realized that "someone was in the house tearing things apart. It sounded like the noises of clanging pot and pans." Scared, she thought that if she just laid still and quiet, they would not know she was awake and come upstairs for them. She must have laid there, scared, still and quiet, listening to the intruders until she fell back asleep. When she awoke in the morning, the first thing to cross her mind was, "Did I dream that?" As quickly as the question entered in her mind, she answered it. "No, it was real." Certain to find the house a wreck, young Joyce walked down the steps to find everything in the house as normal as normal could get. "You know the sound of thin tin pots and pans? That was the sound; it is a distinctive sound to me. I never told anyone about that night," Joyce confessed.

It was decades later when Joyce attended a lecture in Hanover, Pennsylvania, that she had the opportunity to question one of the Gettysburg National Parks Rangers with this memory still deeply entrenched in her mind. Not divulging any information of her childhood experiences or tipping her hand, she nonchalantly asked what he knew about the Klingel House. He relayed that even though the house was in the middle of the battlefields, all he knew about the house was that there was once a woman there by the name of Elizabeth who would prepare and serve food for the soldiers during that period. Now things were perhaps making a bit more sense. Could the pots and pans have been from the soldiers' mess kits and the noise was of them and canteens clanging together as they were being served by a caring and giving woman? It was now clearer to Joyce that what awoke her that night, long ago, was not a dream, but the sounds of a residual haunting from years gone by.

Sach's Covered Bridge

Continuing our journey of the Gettysburg battlefields and surrounding countryside, let's move from the Klingel House and head south on Steinwehr Avenue and turn right onto Millerstown Road, which becomes Pumping Station Road. As you cross over Marsh Creek, look to your left for a beautiful view of our next destination: Sach's Covered Bridge.

Built in 1852, Sachs Covered Bridge saw its share of death during the Civil War. There was no battle here over its crossing nor was there a fight for the stronghold of the bridge, but that does not make it less significant. I have read that in the fields surrounding the bridge there were mass graves for the killed soldiers and the rafters of the bridge itself were used to hang a few Confederate deserters. Known as Sauck's Bridge during the Civil War, both the Union and Confederate army used the bridge to cross Marsh Creek. As General Lee retreated to Virginia on July 4, 1863, he split the troops into two groups; one headed northwest through Cashtown while the other group moved southwest, crossing the bridge.

Sachs Bridge south of Gettysburg.

It just doesn't feel right that a bridge as simple yet as beautiful as this one could have such a history. I had heard about Sachs Bridge for years. Its stories were not numerous, but they were interesting. Sachs Bridge is the only place in the Gettysburg area that I'm aware of that served as the means for hanging Confederate deserters during the American Civil War. It is said that three soldiers were hung from the rafters inside the bridge as a warning to any other would-be deserters who had plans on running away from their duties. One person told me that if you were to stand inside the bridge and call out the names of the states from which the deserters hailed, you could see the faint image of their bodies swinging in the wind that funneled through the bridge. Others have reported hearing horses crossing the bridge and sometimes splashing around below the bridge in the waters of Marsh Creek.

In September 2007, I set out to see Sachs Bridge for myself. I was accompanied by a few members of my local paranormal investigative group we call P.E.E.R., Paranormal and Environmental Explanations from Research (www.peergb.com). Those that accompanied me were Jan and Steve Bolze (I'll call him Bolze to avoid any confusion with myself), a husband and wife team from York Springs; Jim and Joseph Zero, a father and son team from New Oxford; and Stan Wannop and Bob Dockey, both halves of separate husband and wife teams also from New Oxford.

I was a little slower than the rest of the group getting my camera out of my equipment kit. Everyone else was already entering the bridge as I locked my truck and began to walk toward the bridge. As I was only a few feet from its opening, I heard Jan and Bob complaining about their camera batteries being zapped, completely dead. Only thirty minutes earlier I watched as Jan placed new batteries into that same camera. Here she was for the second time this evening, hurriedly unwrapping new batteries so as not to miss a minute of the action. A drained battery is a common problem that paranormal investigators have to tolerate. Since spirits are made of energy, they sometimes *zap* the energy from other sources such as a battery to give them more strength to make things happen. I cracked a little smile and said to myself, "Okay, here we go." As I walked into the bridge's west entrance, I started snapping pictures. I was taken by the presence and feel of the bridge. Its structure was rebuilt and fortified in 1996 after being nearly completely swept away by a June flood. Its floor, its walls, and roof were as strong and sturdy as the day it was first built over 155 years earlier. What I became saddened and then angered about was the visible graffiti spray-painted on its wooden deck. How could people be so stupid, arrogant, and thoughtless to deface such a landmark and piece of history? Through my anger and sadness, I continued to snap pictures and speak to the bridge and any of its possible longtime inhabitants. As I kept pressing the camera shutter, my foul feelings began to wane and again I was filled with the bridge's own aura.

A full-fledged investigation is not what we had planned on that evening, but I did grab my EMF detector from the equipment kit before heading into the bridge. I retrieved it from my pocket and held the button down as I walked the length of the one hundred foot deck and scanned for any sign of a ghostly presence. For the entire span and back again, only one light illuminated, indicating a normal and minimal electromagnetic presence. Clean as a whistle...*until* I made an about face for another sweep. In one quick, short, and unanswered blip, all five lights flashed for a brief second or two. Did someone just pass by me, exiting the bridge as I turned back into the bridge? I stopped in place and began a series of questions.

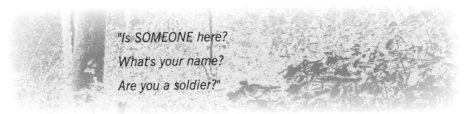

"Is SOMEONE here?
What's your name?
Are you a soldier?"

The meter remained dim with only one light illuminated. That will teach me to not be prepared. Where was my Boy Scout training? I should have been paired up with another investigator using a camera or camcorder to confirm my EMF readings and perhaps capture a passing residual spirit.

Back to the digital camera, I began getting visible orbs on the photos. Jan had just mentioned that she thought she heard someone walking up behind her, but found all of us at the other end of the bridge. Reviewing the recent photographs, there were orbs to back up her claim. My first inclination was to believe I was capturing rain, moisture, or bugs, but no one else was getting them and I then began to change my thought process. I asked Bob and Jan to stand beside me with their cameras so we could all commence taking photos of the same area at the same time to confirm any rain or bugs that might be destroying the possibility that the bridge was to offer us something paranormal. With the barrage of camera flashes in a matter of minutes, we were unable to locate a single bug and, with no wind or even a slight breeze, there were no raindrops making their way into the bridge. I determined that what I was capturing were spirit orbs. Later, Allen Gross, a well know paranormal investigator, reviewed the photos and supported my belief.

Since the other digital cameras were not capturing anything out of the ordinary, I then had another thought. It seemed as if most of the orbs I had captured on film were around Bob and Jan. I had them return to the southern half of the bridge and asked Bolze to join me with his camcorder. With his camera rolling, I began snapping pictures again. For the first minute or two as I took about half a dozen photos, I captured nothing. Reviewing the next two photos, I could see a clear and obvious *orb* moving in my direction and announced my findings. Later that night, as Bolze reviewed his recording that had used infrared lighting, he realized that he too had captured the orb moving in our direction.

It was obvious to me that we were going to have to hold a full-scaled investigation vigil at Sachs Bridge. So with that said, let's jump forward to the evening of October 26, 2007. I didn't even give it a thought as to the time of year, just that I wanted to get to the investigation before winter set in. The night was clear and a slight occasional breeze kept any late season bugs away from the area. The moon had risen high enough to peek over the tree line and provide all the light that we needed to avoid the use for flashlights. Not only was it a full moon, but it was also the Saturday before Halloween. Surprisingly, it wasn't too crowded even though I did get a little nervous when I heard the beeping of the tour bus that was backing down the lane. Bouncing out of the bus was a tour guide and about a dozen tourists with cameras hoping this would be their lucky night in which they would capture an orb, a cloud of misty ectoplasm, or even hear the galloping horses racing across the bridge. As the crowd gathered around their guide in the center of the bridge, I listened from a distance as he told the stories of the Confederate soldiers that were hung here after being captured as deserters and of the people who witnessed hearing horses crossing the water as others crossed on the bridge. It was just at the point in his spiel when he mentioned the three men who were hung there that I broke the darkness by taking a picture in their direction. From my vantage point, I was able to capture the crowd of tourists as well as the opening of the bridge...where there were three orbs hovering just below the rafters. This was one of those times that made me stop in my tracks and ponder the entire situation. The picture by itself was not overly impressive, but adding to that what was going on and being said at that moment made it seem a bit more credible.

The bus group hung around for only about fifteen minutes, but there was still a constant changeover of other tourists with one thing in common—a chance to be scared or famous. Since it was obvious again that we were not going to have the opportunity to setup in groups under the cover of the bridge and try to make contact with some lost soldiers, we took a walk up the hill. One of the other interesting parts of the Sachs Bridge experience that many people are unaware of is the field hospital just a few hundred yards up the hill on the other side of the bridge.

It is the beautiful house on the hill a few hundred feet off the road known as the John Socks (Sachs) Farm and Mill where wounded Confederate General John Hood passed through on his way to the Plank Farm. As we lined up on the road in front of the house, we began banging away at the cameras. We kept track of the temperature as well as any EMF readings, but little changed from what was noted in the base readings. Stan and Joe did report that there was one area downhill from the house that recorded odd EMF readings, but I would hate to make special note of it since we were close to an overhead electric line in that area. All other areas were quiet and the temperature maintained fifty-five degrees with a slight three-degree fluctuation.

A few days later, when I had the chance to review my photos, there were fourteen photos that I wanted to share with Allen Gross. I posted them up on our website for his review and was pleased with his comments and opinions, two in particular.

The first was of the John Socks Farm where an orb was captured flying across the lawn. This orb was in full motion

John Socks (Sachs) Mill located just up the road from Sachs Bridge was used as a Civil War Hospital in July of 1863.

causing a bright solid streak of light spanning approximately eighty feet. The second picture that captured Allen's attention was from inside the bridge. I took the photo from nearly midway inside the bridge looking to the west exit. A group of people had gathered near the end of the bridge and a cloud of ectoplasm had begun to form over them near the rafters. The timing of this photo was just at that point, what a lucky shot.

In my profession as an innkeeper, I find myself talking with people from all over the world. Many of them want to know about Gettysburg and a fair percentage of them are interested in hearing about the ghosts and haunted places. Some of them will even tell me about their personal ghostly encounters, but I find it most interesting when one of the locals want to tell me about their experience, especially when it was not something they expected or even wanted to experience. This brings to mind a phone call I received one evening from a neighbor.

My neighbor, Jim, called and asked if I had a few minutes, which of course I did. He began the conversation by telling me that he was at a local diner for breakfast the other day and overheard a conversation between another customer and a waitress. The customer was a truck driver for a lumber distributor in Maryland and, as part of his normal route, he regularly drove north on Route 15 through Gettysburg and onto Route 30 through New Oxford. The waitress made the comment how she had heard on the radio that traffic on Route 15 had been shutdown earlier that morning due to another truck accident. Jim said that what caught his attention was the trucker's reply. Jim heard him say, "I can tell you exactly why there are so many truck accidents on that stretch of highway. It's because of the ghosts." The waitress was obviously surprised and intrigued by his reply and asked what he meant. He went on to say that it was known by most of the drivers taking Route 15 to be careful in the area north of Steinwehr Avenue. "If you look at the road in that area, you will see a lot of tire marks where a driver has locked up his breaks in an attempt to keep from hitting a soldier that is walking across the highway," he said. "Most of the time, the driver is able to keep control of his rig, but once in awhile, he'll lose control and go off the road or hit another vehicle," he explained.

I can confirm that truck accidents are a common occurrence on Route 15, but until then, I didn't know why. With this new story and testimonial, I took a drive on Route 15 and sure enough, that stretch of road had several trucks-sized tire skid marks. Even though I had not personally seen anyone crossing the highway there, it wouldn't surprise me...*since that very stretch of highway cuts through the battlefield as it circles around Gettysburg.* But not too far from there, my wife and I did have a similar experience.

One evening in November, we were driving home from Gettysburg on Route 30 and were about three miles east of Gettysburg. It was a damp, misty, cool autumn evening about two hours after sunset. There were a few other cars about a quarter mile ahead of us as we approached a turn in the road. As we approached the turn, a large thick bank of fog appeared across the road. There was another car approaching from the opposite direction and the fog seemed to light up as if someone switched on a half dozen floodlights. As we approached the turn in the road and the bank of fog, a series of horizontal and vertical lines appeared in or on the fog. It appeared as if I was looking at a wall with a projected image on it. I had never seen fog that dense and that brightly lit before.

As we got closer to the fog, I could see that the lines were moving across the road from left to right. My thought was that I was seeing utility poles reflected onto the fog. At that moment, we entered the fog bank and passed through it as quickly as we entered it, all in a matter of two or three seconds. What I thought I saw began to take another shape in my mind. Slightly startled, Tina looked over at me and asked, "Did you just see a train cross the road?" A light went on in my head, "Oh my God, yes. I saw something, is that what it was?" I replied. "Yes, it was a train," she repeated. How could there be a train here when there are no train tracks crossing the road and only one track running parallel with the road? I then remembered one of the local historians telling me that the train tracks running between Gettysburg and New Oxford used to cross the road several times between the towns. "I wonder if that was one of those old crossing areas," I pondered aloud. We had nothing else to discuss for the remainder of our trip home. It's absolutely amazing how a person can be silenced by a paranormal occurrence... even when the person seeks out such occurrences.

The Haunted Castles of New Oxford

L ess than ten miles east from the square in Gettysburg on Route 30 is the small quaint town of New Oxford. Known first as Oxford Towne, it was laid out in lots by Henry Kuhn in 1792. At that time, Kuhn's apportioned lots were sold as tickets for ten dollars each. In 1845, Dr. M. D. G. Pfeiffer founded the New Oxford College and Medical Institute, more familiarly known as Dr. Pfeiffer's College, which flourished only a few decades and will be discussed later in the book. New Oxford has always been the county's leader in industry with its mills, brickyards, and shoe factories. Of course, New Oxford's location on the Philadelphia Pittsburgh Pike (Route 30) and having a railway stop gave it a huge advantage.

Golden Lane Antique Gallery

Today, New Oxford is known as "The Antiques Capital of Central Pennsylvania." The town boasts over five hundred antiques dealers, most of them sharing space in the nearly half dozen co-ops scattered throughout town. One of those co-ops is Golden Lane Antique Gallery located at 11 North Water Street (www.goldenlaneantiques.com). The building was initially built in 1899 as the Livingston Shoe Factory. Adjacent to the factory, on the corner of Water Street and Lincoln Way West, is a beautiful Victorian house that today is known as the Livingston House, but previously was known as Seven Gables. The factory was a major manufacturer of

Golden Lane Antique Gallery in New Oxford has its origins as a local shoe factory.

shoes specializing in baby and children's shoes. Today the factory is a thriving antiques mall with approximately one hundred dealers, each parsed off into their own lot, sharing the 30,000 square feet of the building. It is not only the space that these dealers are sharing at Golden Lane...*they are also sharing stories of their paranormal experiences in the old shoe factory*.

Both customers and staff have witnessed encounters with spirits. As I was visiting one day, one of the clerks recounted the day when a customer came to share their experience. As the clerk tells it, it was a slow day for business. There was only one customer strolling through the booths on the second floor of the antiques mall. The customer was inspecting an object on a dresser when he noticed movement in the dresser mirror out of his peripheral vision. He looked up into the mirror and saw an elderly woman in the mirror behind him. Assuming the woman was the clerk, he turned around to ask her a question about the object he was inspecting—only to find that there was no one behind him. In fact, there was no one on the entire floor. Quickly and nervously, he placed the object back onto the dresser and made his way downstairs toward front door. Just before exiting, he stopped long enough to describe his un-nerving experience, a residual haunting.

He explained that he was a rational and educated man and until then, did not believe in ghosts. The clerk was interested in the man's story, but was not overly surprised. She asked him if he could describe the woman that he saw in the mirror. He replied that he saw her very clearly – that he did not

A mirror in Golden Lane that supposedly produced the image of a ghost.

imagine it – and then proceeded to describe the woman in the mirror. With his thorough description, the clerk informed him that whom he had just described was the owner of the booth in which he was shopping. "Oh," he said, "but where did she go so quickly?" The clerk responded, "She died in a car accident a few weeks ago."

It is stories like this that prompted P.E.E.R. to perform an investigation at Golden Lane Antique Gallery. During this investigation, several photos were taken because another investigator had just announced that his EMF detector was picking up a strong reading that suddenly appeared. One of these photos captured an orb where the investigator with

A PEER investigator points to the location where he picked up an anomalous EMF reading. The photo shows a captured orb where the investigator with the EMF detector pointed to and stated, "Right here." This is a perfect example of multiple investigators and equipment detecting the same anomaly.

An unexplainable shadow on the floor that continues up the wall and ceiling. This photo is really weird and puzzling. My first thought was that the carpet was water stained. Then I thought perhaps there was a big shadow from the camera flash since it went up the wall and onto the ceiling. Take a closer look. A water stain is not going to go up the wall and onto the ceiling in this fashion and a shadow is not going to be behind the investigator. Also, if it was a shadow caused by the camera flash, where is the object causing the shadow? The camera that was used did not have a separate or distant flash. You can also see that the investigator was picking up an increased EMF reading at that very moment and that we captured a moving orb in the same photo.

the EMF detector pointed to and stated, "Right here." This is a perfect example of multiple investigators and equipment detecting the same anomaly.

While reviewing another photo, my first thought was that the carpet was water stained. Then I thought perhaps there was a big shadow from the camera flash since it went up the wall and onto the ceiling. Take a closer look at that photo. A water stain is not going to go up the wall and onto the ceiling in this fashion and a shadow is not going to be behind the investigator. Also, if it was a shadow caused by the camera flash, where is the object causing the shadow? The camera that was used did not have a separate or distanced flash. You can also see that the investigator was picking up an increased EMF reading at that very moment and we captured a moving orb in the same photo.

Encounters in this building were not limited to the camera and EMF detectors. Their own security video cameras have been known to go haywire and record an ectoplasmic-like mist. About a year before the August 2005 investigation, two women performing a separate investigation captured an EVP during a late-night walk through. Also, imprinted on one of the facility's surveillance tapes are the remnants of the noisy shoe factory's machinery from days gone by. It's obvious that this building holds many residual hauntings.

Eight Castles of New Oxford

The west end of town on the Philadelphia-Pittsburgh Pike was where many of the businessmen lived in their large houses in the late 1800s and early 1900s. These houses later became known as the "Eight Castles of New Oxford." The men and women that owned these large houses became some of the kings and queens of New Oxford. It was they who ran and owned the industries, founded and organized some of the social clubs such as the New Oxford Ladies' Garden Club, and became part of the borough's ruling body. As the decades progressed for this elite group of people, they became tightly knit and socialized regularly amongst themselves.

As a recent resident of New Oxford who now owns one of these large homes, I have had valid personal reasons for

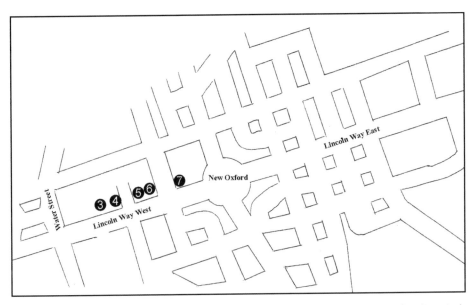

Five of the "Eight Castle of New Oxford" that are reported as haunted.

researching the families and homes in New Oxford. I have spent countless hours researching through history books, newspaper archives and microfiches, and have interviewed several lifelong town residents and historians. Now, I'm going to share with you some of the stories, all verified as true, of some of the men and women who lived in "The Eight Castles of New Oxford."

Castle 1 —
Peter Diehl House

Beginning on the west end of town with Castle #1 is the house known as the Peter Diehl House. The current property owner has asked for anonymity and I have agreed to honor his request by not providing its address or showing it on the map. Built in 1830, it has been enlarged and expanded throughout the years and has a very special feature that

The Peter Diehl House, Castle #1, has ties to the Underground Railroad.

makes it unique in New Oxford. Hidden within the detailed architecture and construction of the house remains a room of sorts that is claimed to have been used only as a stop and hiding place for slaves fleeing via the Underground Railroad that made its way north and east.

It has also been said by several people that while walking down the second floor halls, the air has filled with the fragrance of a woman's perfume. Is this the notion that one of the houses' previous and unseen owners is still walking its halls? The house has always been a private residence and perhaps its least known but most active resident is Alice Diehl, the daughter of Peter and Anna Diehl, who owned the house in the mid through late 1800s.

Alice has been seen in several of the castles on Lincoln Way West and seems comfortable with being seen. You see, she is still visiting the families living there today...just as she probably would have done when she accompanied her family in 1848 before she died. These were the houses and families that the Diehl family would have associated with and visited. Peter and Anna Diehl had a total of thirteen children. Their first child was Martin, who was born in 1825, and their thirteenth and last child was Alice, born March 4, 1847. Adams County itself was fairly young at this time since it was only founded in the year 1800 and named after John Adams who was elected the 2nd President of the United States in 1796. The country was already in the turmoil of slavery and the Underground Railroad was established in 1830—the same year that Peter Diehl built his house. If you would like to see a bit about the Underground Railroad, there is a section devoted to it in the museum at the Dobbin House in Gettysburg.

I have not been able to find any documentation as to the cause of Alice's death. Not even her obituary gives any indication as what she died from. Even though she was but a young child when she died, her spirit has appeared as that of a young girl around the age of eight or nine. Lincoln Way West is her neighborhood and in 1848 there were not many houses in this end of town. Back then it was just a dirt road running through town known as the Philadelphia-Pittsburgh Pike. Even though some of the houses that are present today did not exist in the mid 1800s, there were other houses there, which Alice could have visited. So today, Alice visits the houses on Lincoln Way West as an intelligent spirit. She is not grounded to these other houses, but in visitation. She is a ghost who has been seen on more than one occasion and she is one who still interacts with the current residents, tourists, and visitors of New Oxford; and yes, with me. As we walk the streets of New Oxford and I tell you of some of the town's stories, some of the encounters with Alice will be revealed as she makes her presence known in several of New Oxford's Castles.

Castle 5 —
Chestnut Hall Bed and Breakfast

How, you may ask, do I know who Alice is? Well, that is an interesting story that begins in my own house and business, Chestnut Hall Bed and Breakfast (www.chestnuthallbb.com), which happens to be Castle #5 at 104 Lincoln Way West. My wife Tina and I moved into our house in New Oxford on Halloween day, 2002. Within a month, we began having experiences that at first, we shrugged off as coincidental, as normal, or just our own imaginations. Once we opened our doors for business in the spring of 2004, these *extraordinary* experiences began to happen to our guests at Chestnut Hall. Our very first guests at the bed and breakfast were from the state of Maine and stayed with us for eight days. The guests had their own preference of coffee and had brought with them several packs that we would prepare for them each morning. She had given us two packs of the regular coffee and two packs of decaf. For the first four mornings, I would make her a pot of coffee using half of each type and then... came day five. She tiptoed down the back staircase into the kitchen still in her robe and asked if she had given me the rest of her coffee. I replied that I had used up the packs she had provided just the day before, but I had our own coffee ready. Looking puzzled, she said okay and started back up the stairs, only to pause and turn with another question. She said she could not find the remote control for the TV and asked if we might look for it when we made up their room. I assured her we would find it and place it on the TV. Later that day, Tina was making up the room, but could not find the remote control anywhere, and asked me to look around as well. She had also changed the sheets and completely made up the bed thinking it may be lost in the blankets. As I was about to leave the room I saw it on top of the TV. As I grabbed for it, I realized it was the guest's cell phone, not the remote control. I called Tina and showed it to her explaining that she must have the TV remote control in her pocketbook thinking it was her cell phone.

The next morning when we saw them, I told her what I found and asked her to check her cell phone in her pocketbook. She claimed she had already thought about that and checked, but still no remote. Later that day, she came to us sheepishly, to say she had found the remote control. Not only had she found the remote, but she also found the two missing packs of coffee. She said that she just had the feeling that she should look under the mattress. As she did so, there, just a few inches from the edge of the bed, she found all three items "tucked" between the mattress and box spring. At that point, we were all standing there with eyes wide open. Was someone playing tricks on us? Were they going to do this with all our guests? These questions were racing through my mind. I guess I did not really mind as long as the tricks remained harmless. At this point, all we could do was speculate that the trickster was a neighbor girl who did not belong to our house. We had heard from several neighbors about a little girl who was seen looking out the bedroom windows at the house next door, another of The Eight Castles.

It wasn't until December of that same year when we had a group of women return to the bed and breakfast for their second weekend stay. The four women booked three of the rooms, one of them in each of the single rooms and two of them sharing the two-room Mahogany Suite. Half way through their stay, they were already talking about their next visit in the spring. They wanted to make sure they stayed at Chestnut Hall and saw New Oxford during all four seasons.

On Sunday morning, three of the women were sitting in the living room, waking up with their first cup of coffee, while they waited for the last of their group to come down for breakfast. I made my way from the kitchen to greet them and chat a bit. The discussion was the usual, lighthearted and fun. One of the women who was sharing the suite asked if I knew much about the history of the house and the families who had lived here. I told her that we had done a lot of research and knew all about the house and the founding family. Then she took me by surprise: "*So then tell us about the* **GHOSTS** *in the house.*" I asked her what she meant, what had happened? At this point, the other two women stopped in their tracks and were wide eyed with disbelief, hearing this for the first time.

She explained that she had slept on the trundle bed in the front room of the Mahogany Suite, lying on her side facing the wall. "I awoke in the middle of the night with the feeling that someone was behind me, watching me, and then tapped me on my shoulder. I just assumed it was my roommate. I rolled over to face the door and there, in the middle of the room, stood a young girl," she recounted. She described the young girl as having ringlets in her hair that hung down the side of her face and she was wearing a long hoop or puffy type dress. "The girl looked at me as if to acknowledge me, then turned and walked out through the closed door."

My feelings were mixed; I was feeling surprise and bewilderment, yet a familiarity. I simply replied, "It was probably the little girl from next door."

As the four women were preparing to checkout, without hesitation they booked their next stay for May of 2005. They also asked if it would be okay if they discussed their experience with their psychic medium acquaintance, Allyson Walsh. They also asked if they could bring her with them on their next visit. In unison, Tina and I replied, "Sure, yes," we had no problems if they brought her along on their next visit. We would be delighted to have her visit so we could share our own experiences and maybe get some answers.

Allyson Walsh and her identical twin sister Adele would become frequent visitors to Chestnut Hall, New Oxford, and Gettysburg. They would also become a guest participant in paranormal investigations with P.E.E.R., so let me take this opportunity to give you a little info on them as it appears on their website (www.psy-denticaltwins.com).

Psychic mediums, Allyson Walsh and Adele Nichols have known of their abilities since they were four-years-old. Growing up on a farm in Gambrills, Maryland, they saw spirits both human and animal. This was first evidenced by the girls and their parents when an uncle, Marvin, passed away and appeared speaking to them in broad daylight two weeks later, as if he were still alive. Growing into adults, symbols, a form of language, dominated how each twin "sees" the world, both physical and astral. Allyson and Adele work professionally as psychic mediums, educators, and motivational speakers. Besides bringing through "evidence" of names of relatives, friends, and loved ones to groups and audiences, physical phenomena have been demonstrated numerous times, not only on radio shows, but television as well.

Back at Chestnut Hall, the four women did return in May and they brought Allyson with them. During this visit, Allyson held a group platform reading for the women and provided some helpful and accurate information about our house. She also confirmed some of the names, which coincided with the house's and family's history. A few months later, Allyson returned with her sister Adele. They stayed several nights at Chestnut Hall while they were attending the "Celebration of Life Expo" and working with the New Visions Books and Gifts store, a half hour down the road in York, Pennsylvania.

It was during this visit that we first heard the name of our ghost, Alice. Upon their check-in, we offered them two rooms instead of sharing the Mahogany Suite, but they declined, wishing to share the Suite. I led the way to their suite, carrying their overnight bags. Upon entering the room, I started to mention that they knew where everything was, but I stopped in my tracks realizing they had not followed me into the suite. Looking for them in the front sitting room, I found Allyson and Adele standing in the hallway near the door, gazing around with a half-smile on their faces. "What?" I asked. "She's already here," said Allyson. "Alice," chimed in

Adele. "I keep hearing her name. Her name is Alice. Do you know a girl named Alice? Does that name mean anything to you? Was there an Alice associated here or next door?" Adele raddled off these questions in a hurry as if not to wait for an immediate answer, but rather to receive a collective yes or no. "Not to me," I replied, "but then again, I don't know very much about the house next door, only that there was supposedly a little girl who died there a long time ago according to neighbors." "We'll work on her," said Allyson with a soft chuckle in her voice. "We have some spare time this visit."

With this new information, Tina and I found our way back to the Adams County Historical Society, searching through the newspaper archives and microfiche in an attempt to *find* Alice. Our initial searches were for an Alice Hersh, thinking that she was with some of the first families in the house next door but all our leads and searches led us nowhere. Then, we realized that prior to the 1900s, Lincoln Way West was called Pitt Street. We began an online newspaper search for the name Alice, with a Pitt Street address in New Oxford. Bingo, we got one hit! It was for the death of Alice Diehl, daughter of Peter and Anna Diehl. If it were not for Allyson and Adele giving us that name, we probably would have never known exactly who the little girl is that visits and plays in the houses on Lincoln Way West, New Oxford.

Castle 6 —
The Holz House

While I'm on the subject of Alice, let's visit Castle #6, which is next door to Chestnut Hall. The only information I

Castle #6—a Hersh property later known as the Holz House, it has been visited by the spirit of a little girl on several occasions.

have on this property comes to me second hand and I have never been able to confirm any of its stories. Known as the John Hersh house and later, the Holz House, 102 Lincoln Way West is where I first heard about this little girl ghost in New Oxford. When Tina and I moved into our home, the house next door was empty, for sale, and appeared to be abandoned. Since then, the house has had two owners. The first owner used the property as a business and made a few repairs and maintenance upgrades. They owned the house for perhaps a year before selling it to the family that is now living in the house. Neither of these owners reported seeing any ghosts in the house, but there are reports from other neighbors about seeing the little girl looking out the windows, only to duck out of view when discovered. And then there is the story about the contractors who were chased out of the basement. They were in the basement installing some new heating equipment for the furnaces and by mid morning, they were only part way through with the job. It seemed that they kept running into difficulties and additional problems kept occurring. Across the street at what was then the Oxford Inn Towne Restaurant, some of their kitchen staff was outside on Bolton Street when they saw the workers come running out of the basement heading for their vehicles with tools in tow. When asked what was going on, they replied only that there was a ghost down in the basement and there was no way they were going to stay there and work. When asked about what had happened, they would not talk about it and never did return to finish the work. It is speculated that this ghost is our one and only Alice Diehl from Castle #1.

Castle 3 —
The Christmas Haus House

As seen with the next two properties in this chapter, just because the house might be old does not mean that the ghost has to be from a long time ago. We only need to go back to 1963 to find the ghost at The Christmas Haus, Castle #3 (www.thechristmashaus.com). Built in 1891, this country Victorian house at 110 Lincoln Way West remained in the Hersh family until 1968. The next family to occupy the house kept it until the current owners purchased it in 2002. Living only two doors down the street from me, I've come to know Roger Lund and Bill Patterson, owners of the house and business. From the research that they have done and the additional research of my own, we have learned

Castle #3—The Christmas Haus is where a questionable suicide took place.

quite a few interesting aspects about the death of Henry Hersh, a previous owner, that just don't jive. There are many stories floating around town about the previous owners and a somewhat suspicious death. I am not about to claim that what is documented is not true. I can only tell you what has been written in his obituary and then call attention to the discrepancies and curiosities.

As Roger and Bill were preparing to move into the house and setup shop, they were going through the house taking pictures just as we all have done. The center hall that runs from the front door to the dining room has a pocket door allowing the dining room to be closed from the hall. The first photo that Roger took of the house was of looking down the hall toward the dining room with the pocket door open.

Ectoplasm in the foyer at The Christmas Haus.
Courtesy of Roger Lund and Bill Patterson, owners of The Christmas Haus.

Wanting to change the view, Roger walked to the end of the hall, closed the pocket door, and returned to the front of the hall for a second photo. Upon reviewing and printing the photos on his computer, he discovered that perhaps they were not alone in the house. There in the first photo was an apparition (commonly referred to as ectoplasm) and, in the ectoplasm, some people say they can make out the image of a man.

Intrigued, Roger started asking neighbors what they knew about the previous owners and the house. In their search, they found that Henry Hersh had committed suicide in the house on September 4, 1963. The circumstances surrounding this case are, to say the least, strange. It is said that after he shot himself in the basement, he carried the gun to the second floor, placed it in its cabinet, and walked back down to the basement where he died. This could be a possibility, but another observation that was stated was the fact that there was no blood trail from the basement to the second floor. At that time, rumors and speculation pointed to the possibility that his death was not a suicide, but these stories do not repeat what was written in his obituary... not at all. His obituary in the local newspaper indicates that he died on the operating table at Hanover Hospital while surgeons treated him for a self-inflicted shotgun wound to the stomach. The article indicated that the incident happened at 8:30 in the morning while he was home alone and was taken to the hospital by ambulance. Too many statements in the article just don't ring true or make complete sense to me.

First of all, the obituary does not say the incident was an accident nor does it say the word "suicide." It softly walks around the issue. Secondly, the obituary does indicate that

Henry had been battling a pulmonary disease that had caused him severe pain for nearly forty years. If he was at home alone, who called for the ambulance? If the incident was an accident, then why not say so. If he attempted to commit suicide because of extreme pain, then why call an ambulance? Last but not least, how and why would you use a shotgun, why in the stomach, and how difficult would it be to reach and 'push' the trigger? In my mind, this 'suicide' is still an unsolved mystery. Is the ectoplasm in the hallway of the Christmas Haus the spirit of Henry Hersh? You decide.

In late September 2007, our P.E.E.R. group was asked to hold an investigation at the Christmas Haus. Roger wanted us to try to determine who had caused the ectoplasmic mist in his photograph. It could have been Henry, but there were other people who were suspect as well. There were stories of a daughter of one of the previous families that was mentally challenged and hidden away in the attic. The attic had plastered walls and ceilings making it an acceptable location for the bedroom that had been made there, away from the rest of the family. Also, given the history of the neighborhood, it was possible that there were other spirits that could have been visiting or passing through.

On the evening of our investigation, Roger led us into the house in the same manner that he entered his new house when he took the photo that captured the ectoplasmic mist. With hopes of duplicating the phenomenon, we had three investigators using digital cameras lead the way through the front door into the house. Bill Patterson was waiting there for us and guided the crew to the kitchen where we prepared our equipment and setup our base for the evening. Once

Roger and Bill explained the house and family histories, they answered our questions about what they had experienced in the house. It seemed that they had personally not experienced anything notable in the house since that first photograph, but their two shelties, Tucker and Spenser, had often sensed an unseen presence in the rooms on the northeast corner of the house. Their attention would often be called to the same location in the kitchen and directly above that area in the second floor hallway. We asked Roger if the dogs sensed anything in the basement where Henry supposedly shot himself. "No, they have never been down there," Roger quickly replied. "They refuse to go down to the basement."

Then it was time to plan our evening. We created four teams to cover the large house. One team was assigned to the attic with a GausMaster EMF detector and a digital camera; a second team went to the second floor using a digital camera, a camcorder, a thermal detector, and a GausMaster EMF detector. A third team was assigned to float and cover the entire house using two digital cameras attempting to duplicate photos and get similar anomalies on both of their cameras while the fourth team was assigned to the basement. This fourth team was asked to sit in the basement with a KII EMF detector, a tape recorder, and a camcorder equipped with infrared. Their task was to try to communicate with whomever was in the house. With the equipment prepped and the teams assigned, we went dark. Going dark for us means that all the lights in the property are turned off so that any minimal anomalous lights can be more easily seen and orbs can be more readily detected. Also with the lights out, we can minimize the electrical interference caused by dimmer switches or poorly wired fixtures. I also floated throughout the house with a digital camera and a thermal detector and volunteered to assist the other teams as needed. As I walked through the house, particularly the sales area, I realized it would be difficult to validate any photo anomalies in this area with all of the German ornaments that had the potential of reflecting off our camera flashes. After forty-five minutes, the teams began to wrap up their specific areas and gathered back in the kitchen to report any findings or personal experiences. Jim and Joseph, one of the teams with a GausMaster and camera, had one brief odd experience in the sales shop part of the house. In addition to Christmas tree ornaments, the shop also sold wood-carved pyramids that were designed to spin over the heat of a candle. It did not take much of a breeze to spin the pyramids, but interestingly enough they were not affected by our walking around. I had half expected them to be spinning all night long. As Jim and Joseph were standing still in the shop near one of the larger pyramids on the floor, the paddles made a one-quarter turn, quick and sharp. As Jim described it, "It turned quick and abrupt, stopping just as quickly and abruptly." If it were to turn as designed, from a breeze or other source such as heat, it would have slowly begun to turn and would have coasted to a stop after making several rotations.

In the master bedroom on the second floor, the team of Stan, Jan, and Bolze experienced a little problem with their camcorder. Jan asked if the person who died in the house was indeed Henry and if he was upset about the way he died. At that moment, Bolze's camcorder completely shutdown, its battery apparently dead. He walked out of the room and, in a matter of minutes, the camera came back on with restored battery life.

In the basement, where Tina and Bob were sitting in the dark trying to get some EVPs supported with their KII meter and camcorder, they were chatting away with someone that could not be seen. Even though the ringing of a remote telephone bell occasionally interrupted their conversations, their questions were answered with the illumination of the lights on the KII meter. Tina and Bob explained to whomever was there to listen, to answer their yes or no questions by concentrating and releasing their energies into short bursts. One burst was to indicate a no answer and two short bursts of energy, indicating a yes answer, would be picked up by the meter. They did not get any definitive answers as to who was there, but they were convinced that someone was present and Tina had a strong feeling that they needed to continue their conversations in the attic bedroom. So, it was off from the cool dry basement to the hot and humid attic that they ascended.

We setup the camcorder with the infrared extender and a tape recorder with an external microphone while Tina was in control of the KII EMF detector. Once setup in the attic, Tina and Bob resumed their questions while seated and in direct view of the camcorder. There was a base reading taken in this part of the house earlier in the evening and it was documented that the readings were at zero. Tina chose to make her questions directed more to the young girl who had been shut-up in this room and it did not take long for her questions to be answered. Their questions were designed to have a yes or no answer. Again, Tina instructed whomever else was in the room with them that if they could concentrate some energy, then the device she was holding would pickup that energy and make the lights blink. She asked them to try to use the energy by making the lights blink twice for a yes or positive answer and once for a no or negative answer.

Here is a snippet of the transcript from the attic bedroom portion of that investigation:

Tina: Is Alice here, she is a mischievous girl? *Two blinks after a few seconds pause.*

Tina: Do that again if you are Alice. *Two blinks.*

Bob: If you can just talk, go ahead and talk. *Multiple blinking for several seconds.*

Tina: Good, good. Okay, do it again so we know you're here. *Two blinks.*

Bob: If you feel like talking, just talk. *Multiple erratic blinking for twenty-five seconds.*

At this point, there was an interruption from another person in the house, which broke the communications. After about one minute, communications were re-established with one blink.

Tina: If you lived in this house, make it blink. *No reaction.*

Tina: Are you just visiting? *Two blinks.*

As you can see, this worked well and, based on the specifics of the questions and answers, we believe that the spirit who was communicating with Tina and Bob was not the young girl who once lived in the house, but that of our neighbor Alice, the little girl from Castle #1. Could Alice have caused the ectoplasmic mist on Roger's photograph as well? And just because we did not seem to have any communications with Henry Hersh or his relative, does not mean that they are not still hanging around the house. I have rarely seen a spirit communicate or show up whenever asked; after all, they have their own minds and lives.

Castle 4 —
106 Lincoln Way West

The second property that has a somewhat recent haunting is Castle #4 at 106 Lincoln Way West. On April 28, 2007, P.E.E.R. had the opportunity to spend a few hours investigating this house with the permission of the current owners, Tom and Barbara Washburn.

Their house is one of a kind in New Oxford. It's a Victorian Gothic and Italianate style house with a partial Mansard roof

Castle #4 was a Himes property and is a private residence. This house is also the second location of a suspicious death in New Oxford.

built in 1862. In the early part of the twentieth century, a U.S. Navy captain owned the house and lived there with his family even though much of his time was spent away from home during his active military career. According to the Washburns, it is rumored that long before they bought the house, one of the captain's family members revealed that the captain hung himself in the attic after his retirement even though his obituary stated that he "died in the hospital ... following an operation for an appendicitis and a complication of diseases." Well, now that's a far cry from hanging himself in the attic, but we do not know the circumstances of his personal life and military career. Regardless of how the Captain died, speculation has it that he still roams and haunts this house. Does he wish he had more time and opportunity to spend with his family since he spent most of his time away serving his country? The property was eventually sold to the Washburns who have several children. In the 1970s, during one of their boy's high school years, he decided to move his bedroom up to the attic so he could have "his own space." Little did he know that the attic would never be his own space. At night after going to bed, the lights would be turned back on. He would get out of bed, turn the lights off, and go back to sleep...only to be awakened by the lights going on again. Not only were the lights switched on and off, but also alarm clocks would go off in the early hours of the morning and the radio would turn on all by itself. The captain has also been seen in the house by several people and has been identified through family photos. Suicide? I don't know. An unsettled life and death? Maybe so! So here is another supposed 'suicide' in town and again in one of the eight castles. Strange!

✝✝✝ Chapter Three ✝✝✝

What follows are the details of P.E.E.R.'s investigation on April 28, 2007:

Eight investigators worked this investigation. We began the evening with an interview of the current homeowners who had lived in the home for over forty years and had raised several children in the home. During this interview, the homeowners described several instances of strange occurrences, which ranged from missing items, reset clocks and alarms, to their children, business customers, and employees actually seeing the spirit of a bearded man in a dark suit walking throughout the house. They also recounted several instances when they met with the captain's family members who expressed concerns and suspicions concerning the captain's death.

Following the interview, the homeowners gave us a walk-through of the entire house including the attic. The attic included the room that was a finished space that one of their sons used as a bedroom for a period. It was in this attic room that the son had experienced many (almost constant) occasions with disturbances in the lighting and sounds in the room. Most of the attic however, was unfinished space used for storage and one of those rooms had exposed suspended horizontal beams that were high enough from the floor that they could have been used for a person to hang himself if he chose to do so.

During this investigation, the equipment used consisted of several digital cameras, two EMF detectors, a thermal detector, a digital audio recorder, and a camcorder using (infrared) lighting for night vision. The thermal detector recorded nothing out of the normal. The EMF readings throughout the entire house were considered normal and minimal to non-existent until we returned to the owner's bedroom for a second time. This bedroom is on the first floor and would have originally been the dining room. On a second walk through of this room, one of the investigators lost battery life for her camera. A second set of fresh batteries was installed and was drained almost immediately. As a second investigator entered the room, his EMF detector became noticeably stronger and different than previously documented. Both EMF detectors recorded the higher readings while, at the same time, investigators were getting digital photos of orbs in the same area.

I was then called into the room with my camcorder. As I prepared to start recording, the batteries for my infrared light extender were drained, causing me to replace them. This was the third set of batteries that were drained in that room within a matter of minutes. We took places in the room and prepared for a vigil. This seemed like a good time and place to try to communicate with whomever was haunting the house. With the camcorder running, we made verbal attempts to communicate. Each time that we would ask for a sign of a presence in the room, a light anomaly would fly across the room. It would usually begin out of thin air in the middle of the room and fly ten to fifteen feet through the wall. On occasion, it would come from the opposite direction through the wall and one time, it danced up and around the homeowner as he stood quiet and still in the distant corner of the room.

After a group review of the investigation's findings and interviews with the current owners, it is the consensus that this property is definitely haunted with at least one spirit, which we feel, is the spirit of the Navy Captain.

Castle 7 —
The Barker House Bed and Breakfast

Moving back up the street to 10 Lincoln Way West, we come to The Barker House Bed and Breakfast (www. barkerhouse.com). In 1794, Richard Knight built a log house on this site, which was later encased in brick to represent the Federal style house that you see today. According to the Barker House's website, this house is the second oldest structure in

Castle #7—The Barker House Bed and Breakfast is where the Squire still roams and interacts with its guests.

New Oxford and was a home of the Hersh family for over 150 years and yes, there were many Hersh families that lived in New Oxford. Over the past two hundred plus years, owners have made their mark on the house with renovations and the addition of other buildings on the property. Aside from the main house, there was a chicken house to the rear of the property, a servant's house on the west side of the property along Bolton Street, and the carriage house on Bolton Street that is currently a residence. The main house has also seen changes, not only physical ones but changes in ownership as well. One of the more notable owners, Charles K. Yeager, known as Squire Yeager, married Nancy Hersh, who may have been one of the last surviving Hersh family members in New Oxford.

Nancy and Squire Yeager had no children of their own and no heirs to carry on their family name or legacy. As I read Squire Yeager's obituary in the *Gettysburg Times* dated May 24, 1952, it became clear that even though he had no children to call his own, he might have left his mark on many children. The *Gettysburg Times* recorded that Squire was a member of the New Oxford Hebron Lodge 465, AF, and AM, and of the New Oxford Good Samaritan Royal Arch Chapter 266. Both of these organizations devoted much of their resources and time to helping humanity — their brothers, sisters, and their children. Nancy died in February of 1939, leaving The Squire to live alone for another thirteen years. He died alone in the hospital on May 23, 1952 at the age of 93. Pallbearers for Charles Krauth Yeager (The Squire) were all members of the Masonic Lodge of New Oxford. Many believe that The Squire still inhabits his old house, making him the subject and suspect of this property's hauntings.

With the house being used as a bed and breakfast, it has had many people coming and going in any given month of the year. With that many bed and breakfast guests – all with different backgrounds and levels of "sensitivity" – many stories are told and re-told at The Barker House. There is one story, however, that keeps reoccurring with only slight variations. It seems that The Squire likes to join people in their room and sometimes, in their bed. At least one person has reported seeing The Squire in their room at night and a few of them have gone on to report that he would lie in bed with them. One person even went as far as to say that he laid on top of her.

One October evening in 2007, my wife and I had the opportunity to sit with the new owners, Elizabeth Sutton and

Bob Kennedy, in the main parlor of their bed and breakfast to discuss some of these stories. The house's Federal styling of the period tends to give you the feeling of being transported back in time while sitting by the fireplace. The floors and walls show the typical signs of its age and it would be easy for your imagination to wander. Their guests' stories and encounters were conveyed to them with sincerity and enthusiasm.

I first wanted to know if Bob and Elizabeth had any personal experiences that may have involved "The Squire" and, with a few chuckles and, perhaps, a touch of nervousness, they both replied, "Oh yes." Bob looked over to Elizabeth and prompted her to tell us about her childhood picture. Elizabeth preceded her story by telling me that this was the first personal experience they had in the house and that it happened within the first thirty days after moving into the house.

A small family picture that was "borrowed" by the Squire for a few days.

One of her cherished possessions that had been handed down from her mother was a photograph of the two of them when she was a child. It is a small photo, perhaps two inches tall, in an oval pewter pedestal frame. Wanting to keep it close to her and always visible, she placed it on top of the television in the library. One day she noticed the photograph was not where she had placed it; instead it was on the floor. Elizabeth walked across the room, picked up the frame, and realized that the photograph was missing. She and Bob looked throughout the rooms in search for this family heirloom. It was nowhere — not under the furniture, not slipped into a potted plant, not in the drapery and not under a rug. It was nowhere to be seen or found.

Elizabeth remembered the stories that the previous owner had told her about The Squire and his interest in children and taking things that belonged to other people. She also remembered the day that she and Bob walked into their house after settlement. She walked through the front door and said:

"Okay Squire, I know this is your house too. We'll take care of the house, and you don't bother us or our guests too much."

Elizabeth spoke those words again and added that she would like to have her picture back, that it was special to her. It took nearly two weeks, but it happened. While walking from the library toward the dining room, there on the floor, in the archway between the rooms, in broad daylight, face up, laid the photograph of Elizabeth and her mother. Today, the pewter framed photograph still sits, untouched and undisturbed, on the television.

Bob had also experienced something a little out of the ordinary. There was a large grandfather clock in the foyer that kept the time of day announced by its constant tic tock and chimes. Early one afternoon as Bob came down the stairs to go outside for the newspaper, he noticed that both doors to the clock were open and the pendulum was no longer swinging. He sidestepped back to the kitchen where Elizabeth was preparing some pastry and asked her if she was having problems with the clock or resetting it. "No," she replied, "I haven't touched it." Walking back to the foyer to start the clock back on its timekeeping, Bob stopped right in his tracks. Both doors to the clock's inner compartments had already been closed and the pendulum was back to swinging, left and right, keeping time with its tic and a tock.

The Squire's tricks did not stop with Bob and Elizabeth—he also laid his sights on their grandson. One summer, Bob and Elizabeth invited their grandson to spend part of his summer vacation with them. He enjoyed the month that he spent at the Bed and Breakfast helping to check in the guests, make over their rooms, and prepare their breakfasts. He also spent a bit of his time helping out in the gardens with the weeding, pruning, and planting. About half way through his stay, he approached Bob to say that he was running out of socks and would have to get more. "How can you be running out of socks," Bob questioned. "You've been wearing them and we've been washing them for you. How can you be running out?" In that question was Bob's error. I believe the real question here should have been, "Who's taking your socks?" Regardless, Bob and Elizabeth took their grandson shopping for more socks. Again, just as with Elizabeth's photograph, in about two weeks, lying on the floor, in plain sight was a half a dozen pair of neatly folded socks.

As with many of the properties that are considered haunted and have experienced paranormal occurrences, the Barker House continues to have its share—from doors that open and close by themselves, keys that disappear only to be placed back on the hook from which they disappeared, to the occasional cold breeze that passes over an unsuspecting guest and passing shadows. There is one room however, that seems to get more than its share of these experiences—it's the Laura Rose Room located in the front of the house.

Elizabeth wanted to share an earlier incident that occurred when a first time guest to the Barker House had reserved the Laura Rose room for the weekend. Their day of travel had been a long one so they retired to bed at a reasonable hour of the evening. There are no televisions in the rooms so it was out with the lights to get rested up for their weekend adventures touring Gettysburg and antique shopping in New Oxford. When they came down for breakfast the next morning, they shared a strange occurrence with their innkeepers, Bob and Elizabeth.

The Laura Rose Room at the Barker House.

Does the Squire still hang his clothes in this armoire in the Laura Rose Room?

Sometime in the middle of the night, the middle-aged woman awoke to find all the lights in the room had been turned on. She thought that she was the last to get into bed and made sure the lights were off before falling asleep. She poked an elbow into her husband's side to make him get up and turn off the lights that he obviously turned on for some unknown reason. The bathroom was in the room right beside the bed so there was no reason for the lights. In his sleepy stupor, he replied that he had not gotten out of bed and he certainly had not turned on any of the lights. With that discussion ended and the lights turned back off, they quickly fell back asleep. Yep, you guessed it...later in the night, they were awakened to the lights in the room breaking the darkness of sleep. This time while making her rounds to turn off the lights in the room, she too recalled Elizabeth's suggestion and repeated aloud, "Okay Squire, stop doing that and let us sleep." It seemed to work.

This last story is one in which many of the skeptics out there might want to take notice. There was a young couple, in their mid-twenties, who made reservations for their first bed and breakfast experience, again reserving the Laura Rose room. The young woman had brought up the subject of ghosts in the house just as a curiosity since the house was so old. Her husband on the other hand, commented something to the sort of "oh, she's silly, there is no such thing as ghosts, I don't believe in that stuff." Anyway, Bob proceeded to tell them that there have been instances of paranormal experiences in the house and he gave them a bit of history about Squire Yeager.

After their first night of a comfortable bed and a pleasant night's sleep, the couple stopped in the dining room long enough to enjoy their breakfast before returning to their room and prepare for their sightseeing ventures. On the way out the door, the young man mentioned to Bob that the door to the armoire in their room wouldn't close properly. Bob told them he would look into it, but more than likely it was just the humid summer's weather causing the old wood to swell up and cause the door to stick. While Bob was making up their room, he stepped over to the armoire to see if that was the problem. Upon inspection of the door, Bob realized that there was no reason whatsoever as to why the door would not close. It was not dragging or catching on the top or bottom nor was it even close enough to closing for it to be stuck on a lock or latch. Bob described, "It was as if there was a block of wood or something jammed between the door and the frame itself." As much as Bob tried, he was unable to fix and close the door. As he was leaving the room, he heard a familiar sound, the sound of a squeaky door closing. As he instinctively turned around, Bob saw that the door was now closed. Later in the afternoon when the young couple returned to change for dinner, they reported that the door was still blocked open and could not be closed. As the young woman jokingly made the comment, "Maybe it's the Squire," her husband scoffed at the thought saying, "No way, there's no such thing."

On their last morning at the Barker House after breakfast, the young couple returned to their room to pack up their bags in preparation for check out. Shortly after their return to their room, Bob heard a loud crack, sounding like a slam of wood on wood. Then, there was the following sound of thunder as the young man came clambering down the stairs and out the front door. Bob and Elizabeth looked at each other and then split up with Elizabeth following outside as Bob went upstairs. As Bob entered the Laura Rose room, he found the young woman sitting on the floor shaking. When he asked her if there was a problem and what the noise was, she looked up at Bob, allowing him to realize that her shaking was being caused by her silent uncontrolled laughter.

After taking a moment to collect herself, she explained to Bob what had just occurred. As her husband was gathering their clothing from the armoire to place back into the garment bag, the door once again became stuck, incapable of closing. In a defiant tone, with his hands on his hips, her husband taunted by saying, "Well Squire, if you are here, and I don't believe you are, then I'm leaving, so what do you have to say about that?" The Squire's response was without hesitation and as clear as could be. With one swift movement at lightening speed, the door to the armoire closed with a deafening crack. Bob assisted the young woman downstairs with her bags since it had become obvious that her husband was not returning inside the house. He was so startled in fact that Elizabeth had to go to him for his credit card so she could finalize their payment. So, as I said earlier, skeptics beware and don't push your luck. Remember the saying: *Be careful of what you ask for because you just might get it.*

As for Castles #2 and 8...

You'll notice that I state, the "Eight Castles of New Oxford," but only go into detail about six of them. Now you may be asking "what's up with the other two castles in New Oxford?" Well, there is a pretty simple answer to that question; in short, for the most part they're not reported to be haunted. Well...*maybe one of them is a little haunted.* P.E.E.R. had the opportunity to investigate one of them when it was reported that the owner of the house had the sense that "*there just seems like there is someone else around.*" After a several hour investigation, what the P.E.E.R. group concluded was that there was perhaps one spirit in the house, but it was almost as if that spirit was there to keep the house and its inhabitants safe, keeping out all others. The current owners of this property are good friends of mine and would rather keep their identity private, so I'm respecting their wishes.

The eighth castle in New Oxford is perhaps one of the largest and most noticeable houses in town. Sometimes referred to as the Yellow House, "The Himes Mansion," built in 1804, sits prominently on the town circle offering balance to the other large and commercial buildings flanking its corners. Many people have expressed curiosity about the private residence on the town circle. Originally, this property was built as a tavern, but in 1820, Colonel George Himes purchased the property for his home while he operated another tavern in town. Nearly two hundred years later, this property is still a private residence. What about its ghosts you ask? To my knowledge, there are none.

New Oxford College and Medical Institute

Not all of the hauntings in New Oxford take place in one of the castles on Lincoln Way West. There are some very elegant and large houses on the east side of town as well. It just so happens that in the 1800s on the 200 block of Lincoln Way East stood a Medical College. On this property, the New Oxford College and Medical Institute (more familiarly known as Dr. Pfeiffer's College) was founded by Dr. MDG Pfeiffer in 1845 and thrived for about twenty years. At the Institute, cadavers of infants and children were used in the anatomy classes as well as for dissection instruction. This property was also the camp of the 2nd West Virginia Volunteer Infantry (referred to as Camp Pfeiffer) on October 3, 1898 during the regiment's return to Camp Meade from Camp Snyder at Gettysburg. The camp was named after the Pfeiffer brothers of New Oxford who had lost their lives in the Civil War and the campsite was on the Pfeiffer estate, according to the October

7, 1898 issue of the *New Oxford Item*, a local newspaper. This property currently has several residences where hauntings have been documented. The original buildings for the college had fallen into disrepair and were taken down in the 1880s. It is documented in the 1886 book, *History of Cumberland and Adams Counties Pennsylvania*, that while digging on the property for a new building, skeletons were found...skeletons of children and infants. It is written in this same history book that in the wooded areas on the property, the spirits of children had been seen playing. It was even reported that if there was an electrical storm, the children's spirits were seen to elevate up and around the trees in the woods. These woods have since been cleared for the houses on the 200 block of Lincoln Way East.

This negative photo shows a few other visitors in the woods.

The railroad tracks as they wind their way through New Oxford.

Have you heard of the Bone Gatherers? In the same 1886 history book, there is mention of a group of bone gatherers that made their rounds in New Oxford and other Gettysburg areas. They gathered bones – animal and human – to sell for use in ground potions, spiritual ceremonies, and medical research. It had always been a profession that was not looked upon in a pleasant manner and some people even considered it rather unscrupulous. Given the fact that the Civil War was played out in a big way in this part of the country and the existence of a Medical College in the area, the presence of Bone Gatherers were not considered reputable on such grounds that were and still are considered by some to be nearly hallowed grounds. My attempts to obtain additional information on the bone gatherers have been rather futile. All I was able to locate was a brief mention in a March 1932 article of the *Gettysburg Times*, which was a recollection of an earlier article. It states, "In May, 1872, several German bone gatherers camped in the woods near New Oxford. One of the women took the small pox and died in the woods, on hearing which, the New Oxfordians paid a dauntless villager $8 to bury the unfortunate one." Who were these bone gatherers, where did they come from, and why were they in Adams County? Were they cashing in on the spoils of war and the industrialization and advancements in medicine during the peak of the Victorian era? Even though I have found very little documentation, the stories about the Bone Gathers will probably always remain in the back of my head as I continue to research paranormal activity in Adams County. Could the presence of the Bone Gatherers in the area have had any bearing on the supernatural activity in New Oxford? Could it be that the spirits are forever on guard over their bodies, wanting to keep them whole?

In the same *Gettysburg Times* article, I made another discovery. For several years, I've heard a story about a young girl who had been shot and killed at a town carnival. That was it—no other information was known; in fact, no one was even certain if this bit of information was even true. Well, to my surprise and elation, here it was in print. The following is what appeared in that *Gettysburg Times* archives article on March 17, 1932. "The accidental killing of Rebecca Crist, October 17, 1835, occurred during a children's impromptu carnival at New Oxford. In a shop close to the playground, a loaded shotgun was carelessly left standing. A boy got possession of it, and made this little eight-year-old girl the victim."

With the name of Rebecca Crist now in my possession, I did a little more research and found another printing of Rebecca's fate in the *New Oxford Item's* January 15, 1920 newspaper. Here is that article: "CARELESS IN 1835, TOO. (From the *Herald* of November 3, 1835.) Mention is made of the carelessness of leaving firearms within reach of children, an instance of the kind having occurred at Oxford, a few miles from Hanover, on October 24. A loaded gun was left near where some children were playing when a boy picked it up, pointed it towards a little girl, and drew the trigger, unconscious that in so doing he was sending a playmate to an untimely grave. The contents were lodged in the body of Rebecca Crist, who expired the following day, aged nearly 8 years." How true, cold, and relative that article's heading was then, eighty-five years later, and still is today, over 170 years later. Now, with the name of another little girl who died a tragic and untimely death in New Oxford, I might be able to give a bit more credence to some of the local lore and to our investigations.

100 Lincoln Way East

Also on this end of town, at 100 Lincoln Way East, is one of the oldest limestone houses remaining in New Oxford. Built in 1799, during the mid 1800s, there was a blacksmith shop operating behind the carriage house, and one of the owners ran an antiques shop there in the late 1900s. Other than these two businesses, this property has always been a private residence. There is an abundance of documentation reporting that soldiers, both Union and Confederate, passed through and spent time in New Oxford before, during, and after the Civil War and several of the properties in New Oxford were used as temporary field hospitals and encampments. The Philadelphia Pittsburgh Pike was the main artery that would have been used to get to the closest established hospital in the 1800s, which was located in York, Pennsylvania. Seeking medical services in New Oxford would have been a logical stop since New Oxford was a day's ride from Gettysburg for a slow traveling wagon or stagecoach filled with wounded soldiers.

Next door and across the street to this property lived a doctor, W. M. Swartz, who specialized as an apothecary in a house that was built in 1810. While current owners were digging for their fishpond in their back yard, they came across several bottles, test tubes, and bones that had

The limestone house where a current resident was visited and comforted by a previous owner.

obviously been discarded and buried. Some of these bones were identified as human while most of them were from animals that may have been used in the making of medicines or potions. Back at 100 Lincoln Way East, I have been told that both Union and Confederate soldiers occupied and possibly hid in this house. Reportedly, Confederate soldiers even threatened to burn the house down if the blacksmith living there at the time did not attend their horses' shoeing needs. Needless to say, if this story is indeed true, the blacksmith must have complied since the house is still standing today.

I have not had the opportunity to personally investigate this property nor have I even ever stepped foot inside this house. I have, however, had the opportunity to speak with a woman who was living in the house around 2005 and she described one of her personal experiences to me. Neighbors had told her of hauntings in her house. They all revolved around one of two elderly women who lived in the house in the early 1900s. They say that one of the old women fell down the stairs into the living room and subsequently died from the fall, which apparently broke her neck. It was years later in the late 1990s, as this current resident was sitting alone on the sofa in the living room, deep in thought and troubled with some personal situations in her life, that she felt a cold breeze move over her. As the cold breeze became stationary, a figure of an old woman's face appeared in front of her. The image was cloudy and gray in color, but clear enough to see that it was an old woman. It stayed there for approximately three minutes without moving or having any audible communications. The young women described a feeling of calmness and comfort as the old woman hovered there in front of her for what seemed like an hour. These thoughts and feelings of peace and calmness surprised the young woman, as she actually was surprised that she did not freak out. She felt that the old woman came there to provide comfort and consolation.

Was this the same old woman who died in the house? Did she sense the younger woman's troubled state of mind and wish to console her? Was it her mission to stay there until she had the opportunity to comfort this younger woman in her house? No one seems to be able to answer these questions since it has not been reported that the old woman has been seen since that night. Oddly, there have also been no reports of any of the wounded soldiers in this part of town; in fact, there are no reports of soldier hauntings anywhere in New Oxford that I have seen or heard. Could it be that since the battles were not actually fought in New Oxford that we were spared the aftermath of death's despair?

Chapter Four:

Chestnut Hall Bed and Breakfast

Living Among the Spirits

Castle #5 is Chestnut Hall Bed and Breakfast in New Oxford, where the founding families co-exist along with the owners and B&B guests.

ow that I've covered most of the haunted castles on Lincoln Way West in New Oxford, I would like to take you back to Chestnut Hall and give you a greater detailed accounting of the paranormal activity in our house. In this field, the terms "ghost," "spirits," and "paranormal activity" are thrown around a lot. Generally, I have no problems with any of those terms, except when it comes to my own house.

I guess because the situation is so close to me, I prefer not to use the word ghost. It's not because I'm afraid of the term or the thought that there are ghosts in my house...it's because I feel closer to the people who lived in my house, as if I actually know them. I have heard many of their stories recounted, I have been able to place a face with these spirits, and I know their living descendants. Some of these spirits accompany me on my walks around town, alone, in New Oxford and throughout Adams County. I guess you could say that they are somewhat of an extended family, so if I don't refer to them as ghosts, I hope you'll understand.

When most people think about ghosts and hauntings, they visualize what Hollywood has drilled into their heads over the decades, most of which is based on fear. Well, if you plan to visit Chestnut Hall for a good scare, forget about it. That is not what you will find there. What you may find is a loving family who usually cannot be seen, heard, or even sensed. As a married person, I, like many, have taken vows that included the phrase 'til death do us part.' For the Himes and Flaherty families at Chestnut Hall, it seems that not even death has parted them from each other or from their home.

I guess now would be a good time for a history lesson about my house and its founding family. Based on the deed we received at settlement we saw a trail leading back to the original owners of the house. Many local people told us that it was one of three or four houses (depending on who was telling the story) in town that was built by Alexander Himes. For several months, we would surf the Internet in an attempt to track down a family tree or gain any other information that would be helpful in understanding the history of the house and the people who built and lived in it for the past 120 years. We would find information about the Himes family, but none of those leads would take us to the Flaherty family. The second owner of the house, Ruth Flaherty, was the daughter of the Himes'. We also kept getting conflicting information from the neighbors about who was who, so we decided that it was time to get the facts straight. We made a trip to the Adams County Courthouse and the Adams County Historical Society.

The only information we were able to gather at the courthouse was from the deeds, but that in itself was a bit confusing and at times, difficult to read and understand. There were just too many dates and some of them even conflicted or left gaps in the line of ownership. The deeds also indicated names that seemingly had no ties or meaning. We needed the "History Detectives" to lend us a hand. Since they were not available, we settled for second best and made our way to the Adams County Historical Society in Gettysburg. One of their investigators greeted us as we signed in as a guest to the Society. We explained that we recently moved to New Oxford and owned the property on Lincoln Way West, previously owned by the Himes and Flaherty families. His eyes lit up as he said, "I know exactly which house you are talking about." Without pause, he led us into a study room and informed us of 'The Rules.' "No pens anywhere, no writing in any documents, and only I can search and obtain documents and make copies for which there is a nominal cost, $5.00," he recited. We could live with that. After a short few hours, he had presented us with information we could not have even imagined. From deeds and tax records to newspaper articles and from birth announcement to obituaries, we now had a clear trail as to the history of 104 Lincoln Way West.

We had discovered several bits of new information that everyone in town either had forgotten about or simply did not know or understand. It just so happened that there were two different men named Alexander Himes living in New Oxford. To complicate things even further, both men were married to women named Sarah. Unfortunately, the spoken word was unable to clarify the difference in spelling, such as Sarah vs. Sara. There was Alexander S. Himes who had built at least three large houses in New Oxford (a few of the castles) and there was his nephew, Alexander W. Himes, *our* Alexander Himes, who built our house. Some of these bits of information have created such a stir among some of the older residents of New Oxford that we have had to resort to telling them to make their own visit to the New Oxford Cemetery and see for themselves. I am still not certain if that would satisfy some of them.

Here is the information that we were able to gather and confirm:

The Himes family was rich in history and prominence. Alexander W. Himes was born in 1854. His wife Sarah E. was born in 1857. They married on March 1, 1885. In March of 1888, Alexander and Sarah Himes purchased two adjoining properties on the second block of Pitt Street in New Oxford. The western lot was vacant at the time, but there was a two-story frame house on the eastern lot that was subsequently razed. In 1890 the construction of a larger three-story Queen Ann style Victorian house was completed, utilizing the existing limestone foundation and basement.

Alexander had a very illustrious career in the shoe manufacturing business and later as director of the First National Bank of Hanover. He died at the young age of 53 on November 25, 1907, when he contracted typhoid fever. He died in the very same house he had built. The house was then bequeathed to his wife. Sarah E. Himes was also a well-known and respected citizen of New Oxford. On April 17, 1931, Sarah died of "complications"; also in this very house.

Their only daughter, Ruth R. Himes, inherited all of the family's properties, which included this property in New Oxford, as well as properties in Philadelphia. She was born in this house in 1890, and grew up to meet Hubert B. Flaherty (locally, known as Tim). They married on September 27, 1923 and continued to maintain and live in this house for the remainder of their lives. On August 28, 1924, Tim and Ruth had their first son, Reed; named for Sarah's maiden name. Reed Flaherty died only seventeen days later on September 13, 1924. In 1928 Tim and Ruth had a second son.

Ruth died on December 9, 1968 at the age of 78. She was an avid gardener and a member of the Garden Club of New Oxford. It is her spirit that we have encountered in the gardens at Chestnut Hall. Tim (Hubert) became President of the Farmers and Merchants Bank in New Oxford. He passed away on January 10, 1971, just a few years after Ruth's passing. Alexander and Sarah E. Himes and Hubert, Ruth, and Reed Flaherty are all buried in the New Oxford Cemetery on Lincoln Way West just outside the borough limits.

Could it be their voices we are hearing in the house? Are Sarah and Alexander still calling out for each other as they continue their existence in their dream house? I have determined that the entire Himes and Flaherty families are still in the house. With all that I have experienced and am now about to tell you, I know it's not just my imagination. My mind whirls in a dozen directions when I try to explain some of these strange occurrences to anyone, even to myself. I believe I have tried too hard to explain it away. This is where I really learned to be skeptical yet objective and use my open mind.

Voices? Oh yes, we've heard voices. And not only voices—and Tina and I aren't the only ones who have heard them. Our bed and breakfast guests have heard people talking when there was no one else around, they've heard what sounded like furniture moving overhead coming from an empty attic, and they enjoyed the piano and organ music coming from the parlor when there was no one there to play them...*well, no one visible.*

It all began in the fall of 2002. Only one month after moving into our new house, I was in a garden area that we now refer to as The Bishop's Garden that it first happened. I did not realize it at the time, but it was the first of many experiences in our new home. It was an experience that for some would cause them to sleep with one eye open. It was November and the autumn leaves had fallen and covered the entire property. With the leaf vacuum bag strapped over my shoulder and dragging the electric cord behind me, I would switch from vacuum to blower and then back to vacuum, each time mulching and collecting the piles of blown leaves. Approaching the Bishop's Garden, I tripped on something under the leaves. As I kicked the leaves away, my toe struck something hard. After I hobbled around for a few moments, with a bit more care in moving the leaves, I found a flat granite stone, approximately eighteen inches square, protruding about six inches from the ground. I remember thinking, that's odd, what is this doing in the middle of the yard. I wondered if someone had buried their pet here or something. It looked like a piece was missing from the top of it, like some type of marker. Turning away from the stone, I returned to vacuuming up the leaves heading back toward the Bishop's Garden. Then I felt a firm and distinct push in the center of my back. Turning around expecting to see Tina trying to get my attention, I saw no one. At the time I dismissed it thinking the vacuum strap must have twisted or something like that; today I **KNOW** better. Since then these parts of the yard and gardens have offered up several other occurrences that, as I think about them and consider their relevance, it is obvious to me that some of the family's spirits hang around here. What was it that once stood atop the granite slab? One of these days, I'll have to ask the spirits in the yard if there is any significance to the stone and their presence there.

Earlier, I mentioned that we have heard voices in the house. One idiosyncrasy about the house is its acoustics. With all the room's doors open, a person in the bedroom at the front of the house on the second floor could have a conversation with someone in the kitchen, all the way in the back of the house. Yet at the same time, a person in the living room, directly below the same front bedroom, would not be able to hear the person in the kitchen at all without shouting. During our first year in the house, we often would have to call out to find each other.

One Friday evening shortly after moving into the house, while I was working in the kitchen, I heard Tina calling for me, "Hun." Since I was kneading the dough for some biscuits, I called back, "I'm in the kitchen," but no reply. I called again, this time a little louder, "I'm in the kitchen, what do you want?" Still, I got no reply. Assuming that she needed my presence,

I wiped the excess dough from my hands and set out to find her. Headed for the living room, I called out, "Tina, what do you want?" Again, no reply. Now I was getting frustrated so this time, much louder, I yelled, "Tina, where are you?" I could hear her in the distance, "I'm in the side bedroom, what do you want?" Making my way up the stairs, I asked her one more time, "Why don't you answer me, what do you want? I was in the kitchen making the biscuits." "I didn't call you," she replied, "You called me." I stood there with eyes wide open and a look of bewilderment on my face. "I know I heard you call me," I mumbled as I walked away and back to the kitchen. Over the next several weeks, I would hear a female voice calling for me and think it was Tina...just as there were times she would hear a man's voice calling for her, thinking it was me. We know what we were hearing—we just did not know who was doing the calling. We now assume it was Alex and Sarah, the first owners of the house.

One Saturday morning nearing Christmas, I took the time to clean all the stainless steel appliances in the kitchen; the dishwasher, range, microwave, and the refrigerator. In mid afternoon, I went to the kitchen to grab a beer when I noticed streaks about four inches long right across the middle of the refrigerator door. Now that ticked me off a bit and I yelled, "Tina, keep your fingers off the refrigerator door, use the damn handle." I knew it wasn't me, I know the work it takes to keep them clean, and since I am the person who did the cooking before we opened for business, I always cleaned up after myself as I worked. I have learned to make a conscious effort not to make additional work for myself. With that said, I got out the paper towels and the appliance spray and re-washed and re-buffed the entire refrigerator door.

A few hours later, Tina and I were both in the kitchen about to prepare dinner, when I paused. What just appeared before my wondering eyes? On the refrigerator door, more smudges. This time I could see that these smudges were more clearly defined and could be recognized as finger smears. Now what in the heck was going on here? The smudges were definitely too small to have been made by my fingers. Both Tina and I denied any wrong-doing and yes, again, I re-washed and re-buffed the refrigerator door. Now this had become a detective game. Who had made these smudges on the refrigerator door? The prints were very small and could have only been made by a very small person, a child perhaps. They were also located in a spot on the refrigerator were it was not practical for Tina or myself to reach. They were about three feet from the floor just above the bottom freezer drawer. There was just no reason whatsoever for Tina or myself to be touching the refrigerator at that location. Was this a game, like a small child playing tricks? We would have to think about this, watch. and wait to see if they reoccurred.

The thing is, twice was not enough—a third set of fingerprint smears, this time longer and even more defined, came only an hour later. In the same location as the other two instances, but this time nearly the whole way across the refrigerator door. Knowing that it was not my wife, I got out the paper towels and spray to clean the refrigerator door once again. Frustrated I said aloud, "Reed, enough fun, now keep your fingers off the refrigerator." Hearing the words coming out of my own mouth, I wondered, could I actually believe that the disembodied spirit of Reed, the infant that died here, is roaming the house along with his family, calling us, bumping into us, and smearing up the refrigerator? Could this be so? Yes! Again, we can confirm that there was no one else in the house and we were not imagining this. *These were clear instances of intelligent spirits that seemed to be grounded with the house.* Since that day, almost a year had passed with no instances of fingerprints on the refrigerator, at least not like those from whom we think is Reed Flaherty.

Now that does not mean he has not made his presence known. Tina will be the first to tell you that she has run into him since then. We spent two weeks trimming and decorating the house inside and out for Christmas. The living room, dining room, parlor, kitchen, and all the bedrooms received decorations including a Christmas tree in each room. No room was untouched by the Christmas spirit and some of the rooms seemed to be touched by **other** spirits as well. Some of the holiday decorations in the dining room included tying a thin gold ribbon around the back rail of each dining room chair. From each ribbon, we hung a set of gold leaves and a set of tiny gold bells. It was just one of those extra little items that put the finishing touch on a room's décor. One night while asleep in our bedroom, Tina was awakened by the sound of many tiny ringing bells coming from the room below us, the dining room. To her, it sounded like someone was running around the table and chairs hitting each set of bells as they passed.

Her first thought was an intruder; but the more she listened, the less sense it made. Why would an intruder make his presence heard and known? She just lay there in bed, frozen, wondering what was ringing the bells, but deep down I think she knew what (or who) it was. Why Tina did not wake me I do not know, nor does she. When she finally told me about it in the morning, we investigated the area trying to find a practical reason. We heat the house with hot water radiators so there was no air movement and no one else was in the house. We found nothing that would have caused the "ringing of the bells." There could be nothing or no one else to blame, other than Reed, the little prankster that likes to smudge the refrigerator. Actually, it rather felt good to think that he was still in the house, playing as a young child might.

We opened our bed and breakfast for business in March of 2004 and by the time summer rolled around, business was good. The house was also a busy time for some of the unseen residents at Chestnut Hall as well as the paying guests. Most of the activity had taken place in the Mahogany Suite and now that I think about those occurrences, they seemed to have developed in notability and aggression as the summer progressed. The first instance I recall was of a young lady telling us that the blankets were pulled off of her during the night. The second instance progressed to the disappearance of someone's wallet. One husband explained that he always places his wallet in his wife's purse every night when they go to bed and that he retrieves it again in the morning. On this morning, however, the wallet was missing. They searched their pockets, their luggage, and bags of purchases, but could not find his wallet. They looked in dresser drawers, in the bathroom under the towels, between the sheets and blankets, and then under the bed. Ah ha, there it was! Removed from where he knew he had placed it, in his wife's pocketbook, it was placed way under the bed at the headboard against the wall. How could it have gotten there?

It was a short time later that the disappearance of objects evolved a bit. Up until now, things had disappeared for only a short time until they were found in the room. One weekend after all the guests had checked out on a Sunday morning, we were unable to locate the remote control for the TV in the Mahogany Suite. Knowing the history in this room, again we searched high and low to no avail. Two weeks later on a Sunday evening around seven o'clock, we had made some changes to the room's bed linens and took new photos to update our website. The next morning, Tina called me to tell me that when she was running the vacuum in the Suite, she bumped into something under the bench at the foot of the bed. I almost couldn't believe what I was hearing; it had been weeks and I had given up on getting the remote control back. We had even gone as far as sit in the room and ask for whoever took it to return it to us. I told them that I was finished looking for it and they needed to put it back in plain sight because I would not look for it any longer. While I was still talking to Tina on the phone, I turned to our website on my computer to take a look at the photo of the Mahogany Suite that I just uploaded a few hours earlier. It was perfectly clear that in the photo taken only fifteen hours earlier, there was no remote control lying on the floor under that bench. Where had it come from and where had it been? It was one thing for something to be moved around in the room, but how could something solid, like this remote control, disappear and reappear weeks later, unscathed?

Many of the antiques dealers in town were referring their customers and other antique dealers to Chestnut Hall as they did their traveling around the country. One day we received a call from a man who was on a buying trip through the states and up into Canada. They were hoping we had accommodations for a few days while they shopped the New Oxford area. We had availability and were pleased for the referral. Our guests were a couple in their late 60s or early 70s who reminded Tina of her grandparents. They were a very sweet and kind couple that we were more than happy to accommodate. They were one of those couples for whom you wanted to go the extra mile. Their stay with us was very cordial and uneventful...until their last day. It was my turn to stay at home for their breakfast and checkout on Tuesday morning. Upon guests' departure, I normally ask for their room key. This time I forgot to do so until they were outside. I ran up to the Suite where they had stayed and quickly looked around the room for the key. Not finding it, I ran back down the stairs and out the door to catch them before they left. After all, they were not spring chickens. How fast could they move? Well apparently, they moved fast enough to be pulling out of the driveway as I opened the front door.

Oh well, I thought, we have more keys for the Suite and they will probably mail the key to us when they find it. A few days later, Tina was home for the afternoon to receive some new guests that would be arriving for their weekend stay. In the middle of the afternoon, she called me at work to tell me what she had just experienced. As she was working in the kitchen, she heard people talking in the living room area. There should not have been anyone in the house and she thought it might be some of our friends letting themselves in to the house. Finding no one, she checked the front door, which was closed and locked. As she was in the front of the house, she heard the same voices now to the rear of the house, perhaps in the kitchen, and then she heard what sounded like the basement or laundry room door closing. Quickly, she made her way to the kitchen again, to find no one and all the doors closed and locked. The next day, Friday, we were getting ready for additional guests to check in. We started to go through our checklist for check in, which included going to our key area to get the keys for the guests' rooms. Not only did I find the keys for the incoming guests', but also there hanging in its assigned slot was the missing key for the Suite. I did not put it there and neither did Tina. There were no other guests in the house and we had never shown anyone where we keep the keys. No one could have gotten into the house and put the key back on its proper hook since we change the front door combination when guests leave. No one other than Tina and I know where the keys are kept. *No one other than perhaps....*

Then, there was another elderly couple that stayed in the Suite that summer. They requested the Suite because it had two beds, one in each room. They were a retired couple very interested in the house, its history, and had a lot of useful advice concerning the gardens. She was a retired structural engineer who had worked on many bridges in Europe and the United States. They came to stay with us for Friday and Saturday nights with checkout on Sunday morning.

As they came down the stairs for breakfast on Sunday, we greeted them in the dining room and asked how was their night. It was our usual simple morning greeting, but this time things were different. This time there was disgust in their eyes. They proceeded to politely make a complaint about the other guests in the house. As they described it, they were awakened around 1 a.m. by a loud noise that made them sit straight up in bed. They went on to describe how the other guests must have been coming in late from spending the night at a bar; it was apparent they were drunk and could not remember which was their room. They were making loud noises in the hallway, knocking things over and jiggling the doorknobs to the Suite trying to get in. They were whistling, talking, and going up and down the hall apparently looking for their room.

At that point, Tina and I had to stop them. I looked at Tina, then back to them, and said, "I'm sorry, but other than Tina and I, you are the only other people in the house. We had no other guests here last night." Talk about eyes wide open! This was a real eye opener! His reply was immediate and deliberate. "*Then you have **GHOSTS** in the house because we did not imagine all that for two hours last night.*" A smile began to replace the scowls on their faces. They were at ease with that, and we had a nice long discussion about what had transpired over the last several months. *A lot had transpired...* things that when told, make people think we are crazy or just being silly or stupid. I might be silly at times, but I am not crazy or stupid and neither is Tina.

The following summer in early August, business had slowed and we had no guests in the house. Just before going up to bed one evening, the fire siren went off but we recognized that it sounded different. I walked to the back of the living room to watch the activity at the firehouse through the back window in the living room. As I did, I leaned over the back of a chair at the table. After about a minute, I felt that I was rubbing up against the chair in the library area. As I turned around to move it out of the way, I realized that I was at least two feet away from the chair, out of arms reach. Okay, so if it wasn't the chair that rubbed against my butt, what was it? Perhaps it was Tina, I turned the whole way around only to find her surfing the Internet at the laptop on the desk, nearly five feet away in the opposite direction.

"Okay," I said. "Now I know something just touched me. Something rubbed against my butt several times. I'm getting the camera." The chase was on. I came back into the room taking pictures as fast as my camera could reset itself. "I know I didn't imagine this, Tina, I've felt that before, and I was definitely touched by someone." I sat the camera

The main parlor at Chestnut Hall: take note of the distance between the chair and the column.

down on the desk and got out the Gauss Master from the desk drawer saying, "Let's see if I can pick up anything with this."

Pressing the button to activate the device, I swung around to the chair beside the column in the library. The meter immediately picked up a moderate reading of 2.5. I started to rotate in a counter clockwise direction back towards Tina when, out of nowhere, the meter peaked up to a strong reading between 6.0 - 7.0 and then back down. I turned back to the column facing the wall and the meter came back up to a steady 2.5 reading. I had already performed am EMF base reading of the entire house, so I knew the reading at that moment was not normal. "I have *something* here... let's see if *it* will do that again." Tina suggested that we get the tape recorder and talk to whoever was there. I set the recorder on the table with the external microphone, picked up the Gauss Master, and went back to my position by the column, where the meter immediately registered and held between 1.5 and 2.0.

"If there is someone here, let us know. Make the meter peak again like you did a few minutes ago. Come on, push, do whatever you do, make the meter peak again. Come on." I held myself perfectly still so as not to move the meter, I wanted to make sure that I was not the cause if this thing moved again.

"If" was not the right word, "**when**" was in fact more accurate. The needle on the meter, which was holding steady at around 1.75, had begun to wobble and edge up a little bit. As it did, I kept up my encouragement. "Come on, make it peak again." Shiver me timbers—that damn thing let out a squeal and soared up to at least a strong 6!

As quickly as it soared up, it dropped back down to hold steady at 1.75.

"Keep talking," Tina blurted out, "Ask it to do it again." At this point, Tina picked up the camera and started taking pictures, hoping to capture something on film other than me in my robe talking to ghosts. This went on for about five minutes. Whoever was in the room with Tina and me responded back to us on six occasions. Each time we asked it to peak the meter, it complied. One time it responded in a positive manner when I asked if this was the same person who touched me like that before in the basement or in the garden. A few moments later the meter started slowly to drop below a 1.0 and I said, "Oh, don't leave," and instantly the meter picked back up to 2.0. Finally, I asked for one more acknowledgement and said that I would then put the meter away and stop disturbing them. Within seconds, the meter let out another squeal and peaked to a very strong 8.0. With a big smile on my face, I said, "Thank you." As promised, I placed the meter on the desk. I then said, "If you still want it to detect you, you can come to it." I already knew that the baseline reading at the desk was 0.02 so that would be a safe and quiet place for the meter to shut down.

As I placed the meter on the desk, it indeed fell down to a 0.0 reading...for about five seconds and then it picked back up to about 1.0. Tina and I both smiled in amazement, but I repeated, "I told you I would stop with the meter so I will." I walked back to the table and turned off the tape recorder. It was getting late so we quickly listened to the tape recording. Even though we heard no EVPs, we were able to verify that with each of my requests for a response, the meter did indeed peak with an audible squeal. *Now do you believe?* They sure had my attention.

Later in the month, August 27 to be exact, there was another occurrence that offered additional proof of a paranormal existence in the house. Tina was checking in some guests and took them up to their room (The Mahogany Suite) only to return back downstairs in about two minutes. I was working at the desk at the bottom of the stairs and commented, "That was quick." She (almost) ran past me saying, "Again, that foul smell is back at the staircase," as she retrieved the air freshener. I knew exactly what she meant. Over the past year or two, we would occasionally smell what could only be described as the foul smell of something dead. The only place we would smell this was in the foyer at the bottom of the staircase and partially up the steps to the first landing. At times, my mind would wander off into spy land and get a crazy notion that there was a skeleton or something hidden under the stairs. But in reality, I know that is just silly. As Tina began filling the air with the scent of fresh flowers, I, of course, got out the Gauss Master. Knowing that there was no way for me to turn off the audible part of the meter and not wanting to cause a stir, I waited. As much as she sprayed the area, the smell could not be masked. In just a few moments, between sprays, the guests came down the stairs and went out to their car to bring in their bags. That is when I took the opportunity to fire up Master Gauss.

I immediately got a reading of 1.5-2.0 at the base of the stairs and it was directional and confined to a small area. This was the same area we had an anomalous reading during our baseline test earlier in the summer. Deja vu? Almost right away, I noticed that the reading started to fade. I realized, to my surprise, it was not fading, but it was *moving*. I turned toward the stairs and the signal returned. As I took one step up the stairs, it became stronger and then suddenly it weakened. As I took another step, the signal strengthened again only to weaken a second later. Well, here was a trend. I followed it up the stairs and yes, right to the Mahogany Suite door where it held steady. The meter maintained readings at 2.5.

At that moment, the front door opened and the guests returned with their bags. I headed back down the hall and down the back staircase into the kitchen. About fifteen minutes later, we were chatting with the woman in the parlor, talking about what tours they were interested in taking, one of them being the Jennie Wade Ghost tour. With further questioning about the tour and ghosts, she told us that her husband believed in ghosts more than she did and he was somewhat "sensitive" to them. Once they left, fifteen minutes later, we continued our investigation. The smell had gone away, the readings were back to normal—a very weak .02 in the foyer and stairs, .035 by the door to the Suite, and there were no readings in the Suite itself. Now there's an experience that really makes you raise an eyebrow and say, "hmmmm." Then another thought came to mind, could the spirits in the house actually be taking part in the greeting and checking in of the bed and breakfast guests? Again, hmmmm.

On July 6 and 7, 2007, Tina and I had the pleasure of having Allen Gross, our spirit photographer friend from Roanoke Virginia, stay a few nights at Chestnut Hall Bed and Breakfast. Not only was I excited to have a good friend spend some quality and personal time with us, but there was no way I was going to let him leave town without doing a little investigating at the Gettysburg Battlefields and around New Oxford. In the next few pages, I'll share with you our finding as we passed through the gardens at Chestnut Hall on our way down Lincoln Way West, passing a few of the Eight Castles of New Oxford. During this investigation, a few photos revealed some of the spirits in New Oxford. Allen also had a firsthand mischievous encounter.

The general weather for the evening was clear, no wind, and a temperature of eighty degrees Fahrenheit. While on the sidewalk in front of Chestnut Hall, I noticed that Allen was no longer beside me and I was talking to myself. I had just mentioned how cold it got. I turned around, and

Allen was on the ball and took the picture. Can you see it? No, not my breath, and there are no orbs. It's on my left shoulder. It appears that there just might be an ectoplasmic hand on my shoulder causing me to feel very cold. A few minutes later, I had the same cold sensation and a thermal scanner recorded the temperature drop to thirty-one degrees Fahrenheit. The normal

The author and owner of Chestnut Hall. Take note of the hand on my left shoulder. *Courtesy of Allen Gross.*

In the gardens at Chestnut Hall, this photo captured an orb that was also captured and verified on video. *Courtesy of Allen Gross.*

air temperature was seventy-eight degrees; it was July 6, around 10 p.m., and we were a few miles east of Gettysburg in southern Pennsylvania.

The videotaping during this investigation was limited to the gardens at Chestnut Hall just before we walked out onto the sidewalk in front of the house and captured the next photo. Only five minutes into the taping, Allen and I stopped by a statue that was placed in memory of Sarah Himes, an original owner of the house who had established the gardens. I asked if she could give me a sign that she was there. At that moment, Allen took a photo capturing an orb. In the viewfinder of the camcorder, I could see the flash from his camera as well as all the moths and bugs flying around on the grass as they were picked up with the infrared lighting. Upon review of the tape, we discovered something else was recorded. I actually captured a pair of orbs that illuminated with the camera flash, one of which is visible on Allen's photo. Based on our positions in the yard, I believe the second orb would have been behind the statue in Allen's photograph. The orbs were illuminated only as long as the camera flash, only one frame of the video.

Here are Allen's general thoughts about his stay at Chestnut Hall:

After staying the first night and sleeping like a baby, I found no orbs, or ectoplasm, and I took 187 pictures of the inside of the house. There were no feelings of being watched, no coldness, nothing heavy on or around my chest or shortness of breath. Just Comfort!

Night #2: Climbing the stairs was breathtaking. I went into the Mahogany Suite to change the tapes in the camcorder that I had setup in an attempt to capture something. I had a feeling of being watched while changing the tape.

12:13 a.m.: Reviewing the pictures a cold chill was felt. My back was to the hallway.

3:05 a.m.: Waking up by a sharp punch to the bed. (When something is present, you'll wake up because of the different atmosphere.) I was awake for ten seconds before the bump. Lying back down, I waited.

Twenty minutes later there was another bump on the right side of the bed. It felt like someone was taking their fist and hitting the bed as hard as they could. Getting out of bed (I thought at first that this was Steve playing tricks), I heard the doorknob rattle. Going into the hall towards the bathroom, I heard a tap in the area of the door. Opening the door, I went into the hall, again a tap on the wall before me. I stepped on the hall step and heard my door slowly SHUT. We talked about this door. It doesn't shut by itself and will not stay shut without help. I had no problem opening the door to go back inside the room.

Went outside on the balcony...I kept getting the feeling of being watched.

Around 3:30 a.m., all bad feelings stopped. No more being watched. Nothing occurred the rest of the night. I went back to sleep after getting my camera and prepared myself for anything. I stayed awake until approximately 4:30 just waiting for a picture.

After the first night I would have gone home, not believing Chestnut Hall was haunted. After the second night, I can now say that Chestnut Hall is very haunted. I'm not a psychic, but I know when I'm cold and my hearing is perfect—this was no dream or imagination. I look for facts and then try to figure out the reality of the situation.

Steve asked about the two little kid spirits in Chestnut Hall. I never took a picture of him or his wife inside the house this weekend. All the orbs were outside the house, with him nearby. I went through two tapes on the camcorder in the Mahogany Suite. The first tape ran when Steve and Tina were at the battlefield on Friday night. Nothing happened until the two of them went to bed. The second tape is full of electrical interference.

Kids will be Kids. Steve, they follow you and your wife around. When I take pictures of either of you, I get orbs and ectoplasm. If you are not in the room, there is nothing. Wherever you go, they follow.

It is apparent to me that in this house, which was built by Alexander W. Himes to raise his family and entertain his guests, that over 120 years later, Alexander and his family are still enjoying their home and family here, together. Not in body of course, but definitely in spirit. The spirits of Alex and Sarah, their daughter and son-in-law Ruth and Tim, and their grandson Reed continue to exist and share this house with us. And yes on occasion, our young neighbor girl,

Alice Diehl, visits us as well. Their presence continues to be noticed and discovered here, not every day but on occasion, by Tina, our guests, and myself. Some people theorize that when there is some construction going on with a property that the paranormal activity picks up. The thought process behind this is that the spirits that are grounded to the property become a bit unsettled with the change. We noted that the activity in our house had become more frequent during the times that we were making changes to the house and, now that we are finished with major changes, the activity has become less frequent. But don't get me wrong: *Less frequent at Chestnut Hall is still **FREQUENT** enough to keep us on our toes.*

Chestnut Hall does not open its doors to the public just for purposes of attempting to see a ghost. Chestnut Hall is open only for family, friends, and to the bed and breakfast guests. On occasion, it is a scheduled stop on the walking ghost tour in New Oxford and for the annual Christmas tours sponsored by the New Oxford Area Chamber of Commerce and various bed and breakfast associations. If you wish to visit Chestnut Hall and have a private tour, please make a reservation.

Cashtown Inn

As seen on TV and In Person

The Cashtown Inn, Cashtown, Pennsylvania.

Approximately nine miles from the square in Gettysburg is the small town of Cashtown. What, you ask, might make Cashtown famous? The one, the only, and **THE VERY HAUNTED**, "The Historic Cashtown Inn." Located at 1325 Old Route 30, Cashtown, Pennsylvania, it's probably one of the most (publicly recognized) haunted properties in and around Gettysburg and has been featured on cable TVs Travel Channel and the Sci-Fi Channel's show

"Ghost Hunters." If you were to do an Internet search on the Cashtown Inn (www.cashtowninn.com), you would come up with pages and pages of hits. With that said I don't want to repeat what everyone else has said or written. I'll limit myself to a brief history from their website and convey my own experience at the Cashtown Inn with P.E.E.R. as well as a few stories that have not previously been recorded or documented anywhere else but here, as they were conveyed to me by the owners Jack and Maria Paladino.

If you were to browse through the history page on Cashtown Inn's website, you will find an article written by George F. Skoch. Here's an excerpt from that page:

> As one of the oldest hostelries in the region, Cashtown Inn had served "for the entertainment of strangers and travelers" since 1815. That fateful summer of 1863, however, Cashtown Inn served hundreds of unwelcome strangers, including Confederate Generals A.P. Hill, Henry Heth, and John D. Imboden. Suffering from a chronic ailment when he arrived at Cashtown at the head of his corps on June 29, the 37-year-old General Hill set up his headquarters in the relative comfort of Cashtown Inn. It was a good choice. For decades Cashtown Inn had been touted for its "healthy neighborhood, pure mountain air," and "daily bath" in fine waters from a natural spring flowing through the cellar.

There are perhaps a half dozen framed photos on the wall above the fireplace in the tavern that claim testament to the paranormal experiences captured on film by the Inn's visitors along with dozens of additional photographs in the albums in the lobby. Jack and Maria Paladino, the Inn's owners, shared with me many of the paranormal experiences that have been documented at the Cashtown Inn. Anomalies have been captured on film in nearly every room at the Inn. Bedroom doors have been seen closing by themselves behind a guest, disembodied faces have been seen peering out a bedroom window, and soldiers have been seen and heard both inside and outside the building.

As a native to South Central Pennsylvania, I have visited and dined at the Cashtown Inn many times, but never took the time to do any of my own investigating there...until the night of October 27, 2006. I attended a dinner at the Cashtown Inn with a group of friends. Joining my wife and I were psychic medium Allyson Walsh, spirit photographer Allen Gross and his wife Vivian, among others. After dinner, we were all walking around the Inn, taking photos and reviewing the ghost photo albums in the lobby. Allen, Vivian, and I decided to walk out onto the porch while the others in our group were in the main lobby chatting with Maria Paladino.

Ectoplasm over the author's right shoulder on the porch at the Cashtown Inn.
Courtesy of Allen Gross.

Two orbs above the author on the porch at the Cashtown Inn. Were one of these orbs hanging over his shoulder a few minutes earlier? *Courtesy of Allen Gross.*

It was a rainy, windy night with the temperature around fifty degrees. There was no fog or mist and the wind prohibited seeing our breath.

A few dozen photos were taken during the few minutes we were on the porch. Of those photos, we had three that were of any paranormal interest. Two of the photos that Allen took with a digital camera show two orbs at the far end of the front porch. I moved out of his view for the first photo in that sequence and then stepped back into view to snap a few photos of my own, not realizing he was not finished. I learned that when Allen Gross has a camera in his hands, he is never finished. He takes more photos in a single shoot or investigation than you can keep track of without an abacus. The second photo that he snapped only seconds later, with me in view in the center of the porch, shows the same two orbs a few feet beyond me on the porch, still hanging around.

A few moments later, from the other end of the porch, Vivian got into the frenzy of taking photos and I could hardly get out of her camera view quick enough. In one of the photos that she snapped, you can clearly see an ectoplasmic cloud hovering over my right shoulder. As I said previously, you could not see your breath due to a stiff breeze, and no one was smoking.

As Allen has told me time and time again, there are two spirits that *follow* **ME** around. He believes these spirits are the two kids from my own town of New Oxford and probably from my own house. Are the two orbs that we captured on the porch of the Cashtown Inn when I was there the same ones that follow me around Adams County? Is the ectoplasm over my shoulder, that of the kids from New Oxford? I can't say with one hundred percent certainty, but if not, it sure is coincidental.

One evening in September 2007, nearly a year later, I sat at the bar in the tavern room at the Cashtown Inn with Jack and Maria as they told me about some of the more recent paranormal occurrences at the Cashtown Inn. Only months earlier, they hosted Mark Nesbit and a film crew working on an episode for The Travel Channel show, "Mysterious Journeys, The Ghosts of Gettysburg." Just as Jack and Maria provided them with a few exclusive stories, they graced me with the same gift. I truly felt honored to receive these stories since it is a rare occasion that a paranormal investigation team was given an interview and had been permitted to have full access to the Inn. Before I share with you the results of P.E.E.R.'s investigation at the Cashtown Inn, here are two stories that Jack and Maria shared with me.

After a busy weekend at the Cashtown Inn, a family had made reservations for the General Lee Suite on the third floor. This was not their first visit to Cashtown; the middle-aged couple with two daughters had stayed at the Inn several other times using it as a quiet base for their getaway working vacation. As the man of the family spent most of his time writing, his wife and daughters would tour the county shopping and sightseeing. On probably more than one occasion, he said to Jack, "I don't believe in ghosts and all these stories. I just don't believe it."

Jack was fine with that and wasn't about to try to convince anyone of something that was already contrary to their beliefs. Jack and Maria believe the same as Tina and I when it comes to spirits in the house. We never bring up the subject or discuss it with our guests unless they initiate the conversation and we are confident that they are comfortable with the scenario. Every day the family stayed at the Inn, the ladies would leave for their daily excursions and he would stay in his suite and write, only to come out for his meals; breakfast, lunch and dinner. Near the end of their stay on Sunday morning, Jack noticed the man sitting quietly in a corner of the tavern.

Jack made the usual pleasantries as the man spoke up. "Jack, do you enjoy an occasional cigar?" Now Jack had run a cigar lounge and shop in the past, but with the exceptional puff to congratulate a friend's marriage or newborn, he hadn't touched a cigar for years. "No, why do you ask?"

"I think *THEY* got me," the man replied.

"STOP," said Jack holding out his hand like a traffic cop knowing where he was heading. Jack exited the tavern and the Inn, walked around the front and side porches inspecting all the ashtrays and urns, and then returned to the tavern. "Sometimes people will stop by just to look around and often, they will sit on the porch to enjoy a cigar," Jack confessed, "but we've had no other guests, all the ashtrays are empty and clean. No one has been around."

"Yeah, *THEY* got me alright. Last night I was in the sitting room of my suite when a whiff of cigar smoke filled the room. It happened three times, each time as strong and distinct as the other. Has this ever happened before?"

"Yes," replied Jack. "It's just been awhile since someone has reported it to us, I guess *HE'S* back." I asked Jack who it was that was smoking the cigars. He replied that they weren't sure who it was...that there was only speculation.

On another occasion, four young Southern men reserved the same suite for a Friday and Saturday night getaway. They had checked in on Friday, treated themselves to dinner in the tavern, and spent the rest of the evening walking around the property and browsing through the photo albums in the lobby before retiring for the night. Like all other guests, they showed up for breakfast in the morning and then took off for a day of sightseeing and touring. It was a busy weekend, and Jack and Maria hadn't seen them since breakfast and the dinner crowd had kept them hopping all evening. It was nearly 12:30 in the morning when Jack finally saw them sitting quietly in the parlor. He said hello, welcomed them back, and asked if he could get them anything from the bar. They declined and continued to sit there, not saying a word. A half hour later, Jack again passed through the parlor and saw the four young men still sitting in silence.

"Okay guys, what's up? Is something wrong?" These were a few questions Jack had learned to ask expecting that someone had experienced a little something out of the ordinary. One of them finally spoke up, "I think we're going to leave." "Why? Jack questioned. "I just can't stay another night in the room," one of the other men added. "Oh come on, it's way too late to head out now. for you to drive back home. Get something to drink, turn the television up, and try to catch a little sleep. You can head out in the morning after breakfast." Reluctantly, they returned to the General Lee Suite to follow Jack's suggestions.

Come morning at breakfast, a few of the other guests were curious as to what all the commotion was around 3 a.m. They said it sounded like a herd of buffalo clambering down the hallway stairs and out the front door.

Suspecting what had happened, Jack had his staff check the General Lee Suite on the third floor. They came back moments later to report that the suite was empty and the key was lying on the reception desk. Later in the week, Jack had the time to drop the men an email asking them what had happened. One short reply was returned a day later. The rocking chair was seen rocking by itself and they could hear in the same corner of the bedroom, someone breathing. One of the other men had the experience of someone pulling on his leg as he lay in bed.

There was still one question that remained unanswered that Jack had to ask—what was with the batteries placed all around the suite? "Their answer was one I had not heard before. They had placed several batteries all around the room in an attempt to invite or provoke any spirits. They had heard about how spirits use the energy from batteries to help them materialize or make things move and they wanted to see if they could get something to happen with them in the room. I guess it worked."

One of the most coveted areas at the Inn is a part of the Inn that is not open to the public but, on rare occasions, Jack and Maria will allow a guided tour down the steps into the cellar. Many buildings in this part of the country have wet basements and a few even have a constant trickle of water that leaks into the basement from an underground spring. At the Cashtown Inn, there is more than a trickle of water in the cellar—over one-third of the back two rooms are submersed by a stream flowing through it. A few people have slipped and fallen into the stream and it is speculated by a few people, that they may have been bumped or pushed into the stream. With this type of situation and uncertainty, the cellar is opened only for the occasional guided tour and usually after a waiver and release had been signed.

Ectoplasm or smoke? I think the latter. *Courtesy of Allen Gross.*

On the evening of November 4, 2007, one lucky group was permitted in the basement and I was the guide that led the P.E.E.R. investigators through the wet basement rooms. I rarely go into a building with a preconceived notion or expectation, but this time I had high hopes.

When we first arrived on the property, we parked our vehicles at the far end of the parking lot so as to avoid seeing them in any of our photos. Once my wife Tina, and Allyson and Adele were out of my Durango, I opened the back hatch to start unloading equipment. Allen Gross was already there and had begun snapping pictures. Here is one of his first takes. Is that ecto coming over to greet me or was someone else in the area smoking? My guess is smoke.

Jack and Maria had closed the Inn for the day in preparation for a wine tasting dinner, so we were lucky enough to have the Inn entirely to ourselves. Jack was running late so his manager was there to greet us and give us access to the guestrooms on the second and third floors. We would have to wait for his arrival before we would have access to the tavern, dining room, and the basement. Even though we had some impatient and anxious investigators on our hands, this did allow a few of us to quietly walk through the guestrooms and get some first impressions. Jim Zero is one of our investigators with a good Civil War history background so I appointed him to team up with Adele while Allyson and I made up the other preliminary walkthrough team. Jim's and my task was to follow Adele and Allyson through the guestrooms and record any psychic impressions or medium contacts they might experience. They agreed to split up and go in different directions so as not to draw feelings or information from each other. After about an hour, we compared notes and were impressed with what they felt. There were similarities and differences in their readings and impressions.

Obviously, I cannot provide you with a full transcript of this hour-long walkthrough by Allyson and Adele, but I will tell you some of the highlights they made. As Adele and Jim started their tour on the second floor, Allyson and I made our first stop in the General Lee Suite on the third floor. On our way up the stairs, Allyson stopped about four steps short of the first landing, not even making it up to the second floor. With the brief pause in our accent, Allyson muttered the words, "There's someone here, a man in uniform. Let's keep going." Okay, I thought to myself, interesting, but nothing that caused me to be surprised. We continued our accent to the third floor and entered the General Lee Suite. Looking around the suite from side to side, Allyson made comments on a space that appeared to be of another time, with a configuration not like what is seen today. She envisioned two separate rooms, one on each side of the house. She felt that the room that is used as the bedroom was once perhaps only attic storage while the room to the left, which is now the Suite's sitting room, may have once been occupied by the innkeepers or perhaps a maid.

"I just heard the name Molly and I sense that there is a young woman or girl here," Allyson said. "There's something on her head, her hair is tied back, and she is wearing an apron. I felt her here in the doorway between the rooms," she continued. "There's energy here, but not like the electric field on the stairs." Allyson continued with some further feeling and thoughts, but seemed to keep coming back to women. "I'm also hearing Mary or Marie and someone keeps calling out for Eileen. Do you know of any of these names associated here?" she asked me. I muttered a non-committal reply just soft enough to barely be heard by anyone. "Let's head downstairs to the second floor," I suggested as I followed Allyson out into the staircase landing.

By the time we reached the second floor and entered the Heth Room, Adele and Jim had made their rounds through the other three rooms on the second floor and joined us. As the four of us converged in the Heth Room, Allyson spoke up first, "There's someone here...***somebody*** is in my energy...right here. There's a lot of activity here, it's a really weird feeling...***HE*** doesn't want us here." Adele seemed to be affixed on the sound of someone walking around in the room. "It's a staggered walk, like a peg leg or as if they were using a cane," Adele described.

Further along on their dissertation, Allyson began to speak of several different men. There was the name John and she was able to see the first few letters of his last name; "I," "m,"

131

and "b." There was also a Daniel, who she claimed was not related to the military, and then there was a man associated with the word "hill." "Hill, maybe that's his name, I'm not certain," Allyson said. "John wants to hand somebody coins. There's something special about the coins, it's as if the paper is no good here," she said. Just as a side note, Cashtown got its name because the inn and businesses here in the 1800s would not deal with credit; they wanted cash only.

Allyson finished in the Heth Room by stating that "Hill was here, but he had a fever, he was sick. I can tell this because I feel limp. It's odd, but I feel perhaps he had a bowel problem." Allyson paused for a few moments and then looked over to Jim who was standing by the bed. Jim was in such amazement that I was thankful that we had a tape recorder since he had forgotten to take notes for a few minutes. "He had an STD," she continued. In what was a disjointed comment, she uttered, "There's so much dust outside on the road. So much dust," she repeated as we headed back out into the hallway. We spent only a few minutes in the next room, the A.P. Hill Room. Other than the acknowledgment that a man had used this room and that at that time there was no paper on the walls, only whitewash, Allyson and Adele felt no one there. Another side note: Lt. Gen. A. P. Hill was reportedly suffering from gonorrhea. Now I do not claim to be an expert in the happenings of the battles of Gettysburg and I had never heard this before that night.

While Jim and Adele headed up to the third floor, Allyson and I continued our clockwise circle of the second floor to the Imboden Room where she had little to say at first. Her first comment was something like "there's no real activity here, it feels pretty good here." The second thing she said was, "I feel like John is following me, I heard his name again." As she moved back towards the door, she paused by the foot of the poster bed and commented, "I feel lightheaded." Allyson stepped closer to the door and, under her direction, I stepped into her place by the bed. Suddenly I felt a tingling on the back of my head near the crown and my stomach began to burn. "My stomach is spinning and churning," I uttered. I never felt that before in association with one of our investigations. That was a new experience for me and I can't say that I am interested in feeling it again.

In the last guestroom on the second floor, the Pettigrew Room, the feelings were again minimal. One name did keep coming to Allyson, "Bradley, I can't get his last name, all I get is an H and the word Ford; Hungerford?" she stated with a note of puzzlement in her voice. "We're going to meet the blue," she heard. "I feel as if Bradley was like a secretary, always writing things down and taking messages." That was all that Allyson could sense in the last room. With that said, we headed downstairs to the lobby where the entire P.E.E.R. crew was anxiously waiting to get started. It was time to open the Inn up to the crew so we began with a brief tour of the second floor. Jack had not yet arrived so at this point we were still unable to get into the tavern, the dining room, or the basement.

But that was okay because we could then establish our teams and carry out our specific assignments in the various guestrooms on the second and third floors. We wanted to conduct small vigils in the rooms to see if we could make contact with any of the spirits that Allyson and Adele had mentioned in their walkthroughs. Heck, I didn't care who we made contact with—I was just in search for that Holy Grail of the paranormal: *contact with and proof of someone who has passed*. Jim, Joe, and Tina teamed up with Allyson and headed back to the third floor where Allyson picked up on who she

This hovering orb was first detected by a drop in air temperature. Allen Gross took the temperature reading and photo. The author is the guy sitting at the table getting cold. *Courtesy of Allen Gross.*

thought might have been a maid and had perhaps hid from the Confederate solders. After that, they would rotate with the other crews who were hoping for the same type of results in the other rooms. Bolze, Jan, and Vivian began by holding a vigil in the Pettigrew Room while Elaine, Brandy, and Adele headed for the Imboden Room and Stan and Bob made their rounds with the EMF, thermal detectors, and a camera.

Allen and I made our rounds of the building until Jack arrived only a few minutes after starting the second and third floor vigils. Once we knew everyone was at their assigned areas and all lights were out, we headed for the dining room to conduct a vigil of our own. Allen was already there and had taken a few photographs that revealed a few orbs and had backed them up with thermal drops. We sat at one of the tables in the rear center of the room and turned on a tape recorder that was placed on the table. We began by asking if there was anyone present that wanted to communicate with us and proceeded with the usual lineup of questions. At one point, I felt a suspect cold draft waft over me at the table, and Allen decided it was time for him to get up from the table and create some distance between us. From a distance, he was able to put his camera and thermal detector to work on my location. As I continued to ask questions like, "Are you a Confederate soldier," I deviated from the norm and asked, "Did you follow me here from New Oxford?"

There was just something about the way the atmosphere felt that made me think that someone familiar was around me. Once I made that change in my questioning, I felt the air go cold, Allen snapped a picture in my direction, and he announced that the temperature directly behind me dropped twenty degrees. It was becoming easier for me to be able to tell when the kids, Reed and Alice, were close by. As I just mentioned, their presence offered me a sense of familiarity. Perhaps it is their presence that also allows other spirits to feel comfortable when we are in their space and keeps them from hiding from us. I was certain now that the kids from New Oxford had followed Tina and me to the Cashtown Inn. As I mentioned previously, during my first visit to the Cashtown Inn over a year earlier, we felt that they had followed us then and have the photographs of two orbs and ectoplasm over my shoulder to back up that theory. I spoke to them for a few more minutes before we heard the other groups wrapping up their vigils and coming down the stairs. As Allen and I headed for the foyer and as I approached the hallway, a heavy cold air rushed over me and chilled me to the bones.

At that moment, I froze in place and instinctively began to laugh out loud. I couldn't help myself, it took me by surprise, and I had never felt that degree of coldness in a building before, not even going into a basement. As I took a few steps backwards to get out of the cold, Allen snapped a few pictures and stepped forward into the same space from where I just moved. "Oh my God!" was all he could say in disbelief. He too began laughing at the wonderful phenomenon of *feeling the 'presence'* and knowing what we just experienced.

Once all the teams had returned to the lobby where we set up our base, the crew was invited to go through the Tavern and dining room before they were again setup into two groups to explore the basement. Allen had setup a camcorder with infrared vision in the far backroom of the basement where the field hospital had been setup during the Battle of Gettysburg. There were two areas of the basement that we wanted to pay particular attention to during our investigation. In addition to the hospital area in the rear room of the basement, the front boiler room was also of importance. It was in this room where it is reported that the first Confederate casualty occurred. The story has it that in June 1863 there were some Confederate soldiers in the area for what was probably for reconnaissance purposes. It was not a secret that the Civil War was in full swing. Apparently, one of the locals got a bit nervous with the Confederate presence and shot one of their soldiers. With severe abdominal wounds, the soldier was carried into the Cashtown Inn and placed in the basement. Why this room I am not certain. Was he being hid or was his death imminent and the determination made that there was no need or sense in making him comfortable in a clean bed?

With the first group descending the steps into the basement, I asked Elaine and Vivian to spend a few minutes in the boiler room and see if they could sense anyone and asked them to take pictures, particularly of the rear wall. Leaving them behind, Allen remained in the front room as I guided Adele, Jan, and Brandy to the rear operating room. As we proceeded through the front room, I prepared them for what they would experience next as we moved into the center room. Immediately upon passing through the open doorway, the air temperature dropped at least ten degrees. The full concrete floor had now narrowed to a three to four foot wide walkway surrounded on the left and right by water. Now I'm not talking about a wet floor, there was no floor other than the narrow walkway running from front to back. It had been a dry summer and autumn, so the water appeared to be only a couple of feet deep, but that was enough to place a warning of caution in everyone's mind. This was not an area where you could walk more than a single file. As we passed through this room into the rear room, the stream narrowed to the left side of the walkway while the right two-thirds of the room was solid ground again. Part of the floor remained dirt while the center of the room was now concrete. The original brick ovens from the old kitchen space were still visible in the rear of the room on the wall and ceiling. The first words out of Adel's mouth were, "I don't like it here."

We were in the room no longer than a minute when, as I began to provide them with a brief dissertation about the room, we noticed that Elaine had entered the room to join us. Wondering why she was here and not up front in the boiler room, I said, "Did he chase you out of there?" Elaine replied, "There was nothing happening there, I was bored." Jan chimed in, "You weren't there long enough to get bored," and Elaine replied, "There was a noise and I got scared." I could not believe that about Elaine and muttered something like, "Now I don't believe that."

Later, I interviewed Elaine about that situation so I could understand just why she left her post, as it was so unlike her. It seems that she had her first experience at *sensing a spirit's actual presence.* You see the room in which I had placed her is where one of Gettysburg's first battle casualties happened. This was the very room that other people have reported seeing the apparition of a soldier who appeared to be dying from a bullet wound. I believe that the combination of anticipation of the evening's investigation of the Cashtown Inn, an unexpected noise from the boiler, and the spirit's presence was just a bit too much for Elaine to handle at that moment and her fight or flight reflex kicked in.

Back to the room, we realized that it was not a large space, so we took a few photos, jockeyed around for position for a few minutes, and then left the room heading back up front on the narrow walkway, snapping pictures. As we arrived in the front room, we were met by Allen and Vivian and decided it was best to head back upstairs and get the second group together to bring them down. There just wasn't enough room down there for a group of us to sit and hold a vigil. Besides, sometimes it's what you get when nobody is around that makes the best evidence. I followed Elaine, Brandy, and Adele upstairs while Allen and Vivian brought up the rear. The second group's visit went without much difference, and we began to wrap up our gear and the evening's investigation. For the most part, we left the Cashtown Inn with the feeling that we were not very successful in obtaining much information to verify and prove in our own minds and our own personal experiences that the Cashtown was haunted...*at least not until we began to review the photographs, audio, and videotapes.*

Once Allen and I returned to Chestnut Hall, we plugged our cameras into our laptop computers and began scanning through the photos. Between us, we had over 350 photos and about ten percent of them contained orbs, some of them validating our feelings and thermal readings in the dining room. These shots were of interest, but nothing for us to get very excited over; it was the audio and videotapes that would send chills down our spines and make our hair stand on end.

The evidence that we were able to capture in those three hours on that one November evening was more than we had thought that we would initially capture – and perhaps more than anyone else had ever documented up until then at one time – at the Cashtown Inn. Reviewing the infrared video of Allyson, Jim, Joe, and Tina in General Lee's Suite showed the presence of **someone else** in the room. I can now hear all the skeptics out there saying, "Oh, it was just a bug." Sorry, but no! A bug does not pass through a person and I know my wife Tina does not have bugs jumping off of her. She and the others in the room have been recorded in this manner before and this phenomenon has not occurred in these other videos or with other videos in the Cashtown Inn that night. To support and back them up was the use and detection by a KII EMF detector as well as audible bumps, knocks, or thuds in the room. At one point during this vigil in the General Lee Suite, Allyson sees a light come through the door or wall near the hallway. The light, perhaps spirit energy, made an appearance in the room for only a second and then just disappears back into the hallway.

Allen had also captured several EVPs on a tape recorder during the first group's visit to the basement. Other EVPs were detected in the A. P Hill Room when Vivian, Jan, and Bolze went in for their vigil. Bolze was setting up a camera in another room while Jan and Vivian went up into the room. Jan sat on the bed asking questions and Vivian was on the other side of the bed. The recorder was approximately eight feet away when Jan asked, "Is there any information you want to get back to your love ones?" After a brief pause, Jan said, "You can sit here on the bed." Then, out of thin air, you can *hear* on the tape a voice, loud and near the microphone, say, "I ain't wanted, they'll miss me." During the same session about ten minutes later, Bolze knocks three times on the door before entering. Jan says, "Come on in." As Bolze enters the room, a second EVP is heard. The same voice heard earlier in this room is heard again, saying directly into the microphone, "Hi!" All of these EVPs have been verified not to be the voices of anyone on our team or anyone else in the Inn, and they are not whispers. They are loud, direct, and close to the microphone. Another EVP from the basement was recorded with the video camera. When everyone except Allen left the basement after the first group and before the second group went down, the camera began to focus in and out for a period of about two minutes. During that period, a light orb makes its presence in and out of the room and you can clearly hear someone walking or splashing in the water. The only door that was not covered was behind the camera and there was no water in that part of the room. If it had been Allen, we would have noticed him being wet. *There is no other explanation other than a **disembodied***

person *walking or working in the water.* Also, on the same videotape, we captured something even more incredible.

Just before Allen enters the rear room in the basement, the camera is again running in and out of focus. There is no one in the room, and there is nothing there that should be causing the camera to react that way. Just as the camera goes out of focus, about five seconds before Allen enters the room from the left, a cloud of ectoplasm forms and is visible on the rear and right side of the room. The ecto takes shape – *the shape of a person* – and quickly moves from right to left, passing Allen, and exiting the room.

In another part of the building, in the lobby, Allen had set up a video camera to record the stairs to the second floor and the hallway leading to the dining room. Twice, you can clearly see an energy orb roaming around. Now I call this an orb, but don't get the image of a grayish translucent orb that is typical in photographs. This orb was different and I believe is probably the same energy orb that was captured earlier in the General Lee Suite by Allyson. What we see on this video clip is a bright white light—one that actually generates its own light. We reviewed this tape dozens of times and each time we watched it, our disbelief waned until it was completely turned into belief. Watching frame by frame, it became clear to us that this energy was intelligent. It was roaming around, perhaps observing us. You can actually see it moving behind the spindles and newel posts of the staircase as if it were playing, up and down the staircase. This actually dispels the theory that someone was using a penlight or something else to create the light and trick us. The second time this energy became present in the hallway, it became obvious to us that it was actually generating light, since it caused a light reflection on a hall table several feet away and in front of it. Since it was creating its own light confirms why Allyson could see it in the General Lee Suite and how Jan saw a similar light during her vigil in a different room. Both of these occurrences by these investigators are documented and captured on audio recordings that were made during their vigils.

Several minutes later, this same orb appeared in the same location on the stairs. On close examination of this five-second clip, the orb sort of wobbled, changing its shape as it first appears out of the steps and heads down the hall. As it moves along, you can actually see its reflecting light on the sofa table about six feet away. This time the orb travels only about ten feet where, just before disappearing, it splits into two separate orbs about two feet apart. After a bit of pondering this instance, one question that comes to mind is; was it one orb that split into two or was it actually two orbs traveling together and then split up? I guess that's one question for which I'll never know the answer. By putting together a timeline incorporating all the audio and video recordings, it appears that there was at least one energy orb, a spirit, roaming all over the Inn, stopping in on us from time to time. This seems to have been a spirit that is grounded to the Cashtown Inn.

Do you remember me asking the question in the first paragraph of this book; Are we ever really alone? My answer to that question is, I don't think we are, at least not for most of the time. *In Adams County, Pennsylvania, in Gettysburg, New Oxford, and Cashtown, I believe that most of the time we are not walking alone, that we are walking with the ghosts that continue to exist and are tied to the fields, hills, buildings, and homes in Adams County.* My experiences at the Cashtown Inn are just one more validation of this theory.

Chapter Six:

Bechtel Victorian Mansion Bed & Breakfast Inn

Family Tragedy in East Berlin

The Bechtel Victorian Mansion Bed and Breakfast Inn in East Berlin, Pennsylvania. This view shows a good angle of the turret balcony where a young Victorian lady has been seen.

Located eighteen miles east of Gettysburg, in East Berlin's National Historic District, is the Bechtel Victorian Mansion Bed & Breakfast Inn at 400 West King Street (http://gettysburgareainns.com/tcbb-Bechtel. html). While this mansion is living proof of a lifestyle in the late nineteenth century, there are occasions when the nonliving has interacted with the living. Her name is Flossie Leas, and she was twenty-two years old when she died from a bout with spinal meningitis on April 19, 1907. Flossie's death was not the only blow to the Leas family in East Berlin. Less than two years earlier, on July 10, 1905, Flossie's younger brother Melvin fell from his horse and drowned in the Conawago Creek near their home. Three years earlier on March 28, 1902, their mother had passed away at the age of forty-two, and another of Flossie's younger brothers, William Jr., died on January 15, 1896. How could such tragedy be bestowed on one family? How can a man bear the death of not only one, but three, of his children and his wife at such young ages in an eleven-year span? Perhaps he did not have to get used to not seeing them around. If it is Flossie that has been noticed in the house by its current owners, guests, staff, and passersby, then perhaps she never left her family and this beautiful Victorian mansion. We do not know if William and his surviving two daughters were aware that they were living in the house with the spirits of their deceased family members. In 1915, William suffered a stroke of apoplexy and spent a few days in the hospital before returning to his home, where he died only a few days later on September 2. His daughters Beulah and Sara lived long lives and remained in the house for an additional sixty-seven years. They had been referred to as spinsters and many children in East Berlin would cross the street before passing the house if they saw the sisters outside.

William G. Leas had inherited family money when his father died in 1891, and he built this home for his family in 1897. William owned the lumber mill in town that was supplied with the raw lumber that was harvested from the woodlands that he owned from Virginia to Vermont. One walk through the house and you can clearly see the products of his money in the abundance of carved wooden trim, doors, and accouterments that make this house the Queen Ann Victorian gem that it is.

After Sara's death on March 4, 1982, Charles Bechtel bought the house and opened the Bechtel Victorian Mansion Bed and Breakfast. He never did live in the house and, knowing nothing of the spirit that roamed the halls and rooms, sold it to the current owners in 1999. Carol and Rich Carlson are the third owners and only the second family to live in this 110-year-old house. They too knew nothing about the house being haunted until one and a half years after they were in the house; one of their B&B guests informed them that she was a psychic and that there was a calm, contented, yet shy spirit that was grounded to the house. It was then that they started to pay closer attention to the little and strange happenings in the big old house. As I sat interviewing Carol and listening to her stories, it was apparent to me that she and her husband were convinced that Flossie was still in the house and they were content to live there together with her.

As you read the stories surrounding Bechtel Mansion, like me, you too may scratch your head and wonder if Flossie is the only spirit in the house. Pay attention to the dates and circumstances surrounding some of the deaths of the Leas family and draw some of your own conclusions. I know I'll be making another call to schedule a visit with P.E.E.R. Perhaps we can find out if there is more than one family spirit sharing the house with the bed and breakfast's guests.

It was in the summer of 2003, during the July 4th holiday weekend, when the bed and breakfast had just emptied from a full house of guests. Carol and Rich's housekeeper was

The Master Bedroom in The Bechtel Victorian Mansion.

unable to come into work, so Carol called on a friend to help with cleaning and changing over all nine guestrooms. We'll call the friend "Jane." Carol was hard at work in the laundry room, Rich was taking care of the dining room and kitchen cleanup, and Jane was upstairs making up all the beds. As typical in South Central Pennsylvania, it was a hot and humid afternoon, but to conserve energy and costs, all the window air conditioners had been turned off in the guestrooms. As Jane made her way to the Master Bedroom, she was pleased to realize that she was nearly finished with making up the bed and she would soon be able to head downstairs where it was cooler. Nearing completion in the Master Bedroom, someone tapped Jane on the shoulder. As she turned around to acknowledge them, a cold damp breeze replaced the hot summer air. And yes, you guessed it...there was no one else in the room or anywhere on the second floor. Startled, she quickly headed down the stairs to find Carol and Rich to tell them what she just experienced. Still a little skeptical, they listened to her story, but were unable to validate it since no one else had ever reported anything like it. Well, it did not take long for someone else to have a similar experience. This time instead of a tap on the shoulder, it was a brush on the cheek and hair. Like the first experience, it happened in the Master Bedroom but unlike the other time it did not happen to the cleaning staff, it happened to Rich himself. The only thing in question now was, who was in the Master Bedroom making contact with its occupants? Could it be Flossie or was it perhaps her younger brother Melvin, who in four days would be the 98th anniversary of his own death?

On a Sunday morning, about a year later in 2004, Carol and Rich were cleaning the guestrooms after another busy weekend. The doorbell rang, and when they answered it, a police officer was standing there. This of course gave them reason for concern as the officer held up his badge and told them that he was a cop from York. He told them that he wasn't nuts, but his wife thought perhaps that was the case. The officer asked if they were running a publicity stunt. Rich stated with a note of concern in his voice, "No, why?" He said that he had driven by the Inn several times on his way home from work, and each time he saw a young woman who appeared to be in her early twenties standing out on the turret balcony, staring off into the distance. On the many times that he saw her, he thought nothing of it, just assuming that she was either a mannequin or a person in costume. This last time was different; this time he watched as she turned around and walked into the house...***through the wall***, not needing to use the door! Today, with his doubtful wife accompanying him, he had to stop and ask whom it was that looked over East Berlin from the turret. (By the way, the police officer's wife would not leave her car and come up to the house. I guess in her skepticism, there was still a little smidgen of fear as to what she just might hear or see for herself.)

Several months later, Carol and Rich were out for a relaxing drive and stopped at a local pottery shop on Abbottstown Road. While chatting with the pottery's owners, they told them who they were. A light must have gone on in the heads of the other couple, as the subject instantly changed direction as they asked about *their* ghost...the young woman who stands out on the turret balcony. Obviously, more than one person had seen her or at least heard of her.

That following November, a group of noisy, inconsiderate, destructive guests booked eight of the nine rooms (their words, not mine) for a weekend stay. Some of them took the three rooms on the third floor, which includes the Turret Room where the ghost had been seen. Most of the guests were smokers, which was probably the reason they wanted that room. When they came downstairs for breakfast on Saturday morning, they complained that they were each missing a half pack of cigarettes that "disappeared" sometime Friday night. Carol told them that she didn't take them because she didn't smoke. One of the guests then said in a joking and unsuspecting manner, "Oh, well maybe your ghost took them then." Carol smiled and simply replied,

"Maybe she did!" After that weekend, alone in the house with no other guests, Carol said she would smell cigarette smoke in the dining room and the parlor every night between nine and ten o'clock.

Could it be Flossie that stands outside on the turret adjacent to the Turret Room? Was Flossie a closet smoker? After all, in the early 1900s, a woman smoking was something that would have been frowned upon, and the turret, which was accessible from the third floor, would have been a good place to hide and sneak a quick smoke. Did these guests unknowingly provide Flossie with the perfect opportunity to 'help herself' to a week's supply of fresh cigarettes?

Periodically, Carol and Rich will catch a whiff of cigarette smoke, but it's no longer confined to the dining room or parlor. The smoke can be smelled anywhere in the house, in one of the bedrooms, or in the hall, or even in the basement. According to Carol, this always happened when they had completed a redecorating project in one of the rooms. One night after retiring to bed, Rich commented to Carol, "*She's here...**she's** standing at the foot of the bed, watching us.*"

A young couple checked in to spend a few nights on January 1 and 2, 2005. They asked the innkeepers if they had any ghosts in the house. In reply, they told them what they had experienced and also what a few of the other guests' encountered. The wife had a necklace made of sterling silver chains and a turquoise pendant that she had purchased that summer during her honeymoon in Mexico. The chains on one side of the necklace had become entangled, and no one had been able to fix it for her. She laid the necklace on the table in her guestroom near the door to the turret. On the morning that she was to leave, she came down to breakfast holding up the necklace and asked Carol if anyone had touched it. Of course, they had not, and Carol told her so. Then the young wife said, "Thank you, Flossie!" She relayed the story about how the strands of silver had tangled up on her and neither her husband nor any of her co-workers had been able to untangle it.

Guests have taken many pictures in the house, but there is one in particular that came to Carol's attention during our interview. One guest took photos with her digital camera the morning that she was leaving. There was no one in the dining room and no way that there could be a shadow, but when she showed the photo to Carol and Rich, they could see part of a body, including the arm and shoulder of a person standing next to the built-in corner hutch. "It was translucent, but you could see it nevertheless," remarked Carol. "Another guest took photos in the Turret Room where they were staying, and their photos showed 'orbs' in the room and again, the shadow of a lady's arm."

In July 2007, a sister-in-law visited for a few days and said that a cigarette was missing from an unopened pack of cigarettes on her first day there. Then on the second day, she said her rings and bracelet had been moved during the night and were not where she had placed them. At the end of our interview, I asked Carol what she thought about ghosts in the house. She replied, "Not too often, but every once in a while I will still smell cigarette smoke when I'm alone at night. So I talk to Flossie. I ask her how she's doing and thank her for keeping me company. I would love to see her. We both would love to see her."

Chapter Seven:

More Than You Can Shake a Stick At

The Bolze residence just north of York Springs, Pennsylvania.

Jan and Bolze are both members of the paranormal research group P.E.E.R. and have been mentioned several times throughout this book. In fact, Jan was very instrumental in the Cashtown Inn investigation when it came to capturing most of its EVPs. Jan and Bolze live on Mountain Road just a few miles north of a small town in Adams County called York Springs. Their house is not a large mansion nor is it a new house. It is a modest, pre-Civil War property that has its share of ghosts. Jan and Bolze live there with their ghost in peace and even though they are paranormal investigators, like me, they have no desire to hold an extensive investigation in their home or to disturb the natural order of things and the unseen inhabitants in their home.

As I sat at their kitchen table one night talking to them about what got them interested in ghost hunting, they had no hesitations telling me about many of the ghostly experiences in their home. Most of the occurrences have been in the form of noises and smells, but the one incident that sent Bolze over the edge, had him angered to the point of yelling and accusing his family of mischief.

A few years earlier, Bolze set out to make a kitchen table for their home. He put his heart and soul into that table, and it was the same kitchen table at which I was now seated taking my notes. It was made from rough sawn lumber that looked like it could have been salvaged from an old house or barn. Its appearance was reminiscent of an older farmhouse kitchen worktable. Bolze had the boards cut to size, then assembled them with great care and expertise, and spent several days applying the finishing coats of urethane. With the last coat applied, Bolze went to bed anxious to see the finished results in the morning, but what he found was not what he had expected. The smooth clear satin finish was marred by what appeared to be several streaks and smudges caused by someone's untimely ill-placed fingers. Who in the house would have done such a thing? Bolze confronted each of his sons and Jan about this cruel act demanding to know why, all of whom denied the deed. It was then, with

Jan's convincing, that they realized that those living in the house were innocent and that perhaps the guilty person was among the dead...*one of the spirits that walks among them in their house*.

Jan's first recollection that there was someone else in their home happened one evening in 1986. Jan and Bolze were in the process of renovating their living room, spending many of their evenings and weekends stripping, tearing down, and resurfacing the floors, walls, and ceilings. After a long evening of work, they put the kids to bed and settled down to unwind for a while before they, too, went to bed. While they were watching some TV, they noticed one of the kids had gotten out of bed and was walking around upstairs. Bolze volunteered to go up and see who wasn't asleep and why. He returned to the living room in a few minutes and Jan asked which of the boys were up and what was going on. Puzzled, Bolze replied, "The boys are asleep." Ever since then, they would come home at night after work or out just for the day, and many times the lights would be turned on. They also discovered that they have one of those TVs that like to change channels by itself.

But that night in 1986 was not the only time Jan has heard footsteps in the house. There have also been occasions when she was ironing in the living room when she would hear someone walking down the stairs into the kitchen. Bolze recalled one instance when he was lying awake in bed about three o'clock in the morning and he heard footsteps coming up the stairs and then head back down to the kitchen. Since his one son was working a late shift, he assumed it was he who had come home from work. As Bolze lie in bed, he began to smell bacon and eggs being fried in the kitchen. Not yet ready to fall asleep, Bolze quietly slid out of bed so as not to awaken Jan, and headed down to the kitchen to share some of those eggs and bacon that his son was preparing. As he got to the bedroom door and opened it, he noticed that the house was completely dark and then he noticed that the smell of food had completely disappeared. As Bolze reached the bottom of the stairs, which entered into the kitchen, he realized that the entire house was dark. Bolze made a quick u-turn and headed back upstairs to his son's bedroom. It too was dark and empty, for his son had not yet returned home from work, and everyone else in the house was sound asleep.

Three o'clock in the morning seems to be an **ACTIVE** time in their home. Bolze recalled another incident that happened at the same time of the morning. He had gone to bed earlier than Jan that evening because he was more tired than normal since he had just spent most of the day tearing down a dividing wall, which turned two rooms into one larger kitchen. A few minutes before three o'clock, he nearly sprang out of bed with the noise of Jan moving all the pots and pans that needed to be relocated while the kitchen work proceeded. Looking at the clock and realizing the time, Bolze headed downstairs to get her to stop work, come to bed, and more importantly, let him get back to sleep. This turned out to be a change in plans when Bolze had to wake up Jan who had fallen asleep on the sofa hours earlier.

Jan and Bolze are not the only ones who have been privileged to hearing the footsteps, thumping, and banging in the house. One day they were approached by their eight-year-old son who wanted to know who the man was that frequently sits at his desk in his bedroom. Even though astonished, Jan and Bolze were not overly concerned since they had been given no reason to feel threatened by the spirits in their house. Jan asked her son if he could describe the man, which he did in a somewhat brief and vague manner. He described the man as having a slight build, greased back hair, and glasses. Jan went over to a cupboard in the kitchen and took out a crock that contained some artifacts they had found in the walls and under the floors during renovations. She showed her son an old tintype photo of two men sitting on chairs and asked if the man at his desk looked like either of them. The boy gazed at the photo, then raised his eyes to Jan's and replied, "Ah ha, kind of."

After that, the noises seemed to progress into sightings and touches. Bolze had been wakened on occasion by being poked in the leg and once seeing shadows move over his face in the early hours of the morning. Each time as Bolze rolled over to see what Jan wanted, he realized, like all the other times, Jan was sound asleep. When I asked them who they thought was in the house, their reply was simple and direct, "We don't know." I got the distinct impression that knowing who was there was not a priority for them. It could be Mr. or Mrs. Zeigler who lived there and died in the 1840s and 50s. It could also be Sara Hoffman who once owned the "Tenant House." After all, the Zeiglers and the Hoffmans never did go far from home even when they died; they are all buried in the small cemetery only five hundred feet from their front door. But then again with a cemetery that close to home, you never know who could just pop in for a visit.

There are many other properties in Adams County that are suspected to be haunted and many of them are visited on a regular basis by tourists and ghost hunters alike. Located in the Gettysburg National Park, there's the Wheatfield that is perhaps one of the most reported areas for EVPs. As one of the bloodiest areas of battle, sounds of gunfire and horses are reportedly heard. The Triangular Field hosts a multitude of paranormal stories; from soldiers approaching tourists only to disappear when they get close, to seeing sharpshooters poised for action and photographic equipment having its batteries drained. Devil's Den is one of those locations that many ghost hunters have some initial difficulty understanding, as it's reportedly been haunted long before the American Civil War. When a novice ghost hunter sits amongst the rocks at Devil's Den waiting to see or hear a soldier and unexpectedly witnesses the whoop of an Indian, he becomes quite confused and disturbed. Some have said that Devil's Den was a place of battle, burial, and worship for some American Indians long before the settlers moved into this part of the country. There have been many experiences here that include the small nearby stream turning red with blood.

In downtown Gettysburg, the Jennie Wade House is where the only civilian was killed during the Battle of Gettysburg. Visitors touring the house claim to feel her presence in the basement where she was laid to die from her rifle wound. The Pub at the Gettysburg Square (www.the-pub.com) hosts a haunting from contemporary times. Employees report that the spirit of a murdered woman visits the kitchen and ladies room. Not every haunting has to be from days long past. Death occurs every day and new spirits and ghosts are created to walk this earth. Pennsylvania Hall at Gettysburg College was once used as a lookout post for Confederate sentries posted in the cupola as well as a field hospital during the battle at Gettysburg. Stories there range from seeing the residual hauntings of the sentries to the college staff witnessing a horrific scene in the operating room from over a century ago.

A few miles down the road from Gettysburg is the very small town of Hunterstown. The Jacob Grass Hotel in Hunterstown saw battle during the Civil War. According to the Hunterstown Historical Society, the Jacob Grass Hotel served as Union headquarters, where orders were given by Judson Kilpatrick to General George Armstrong Custer to "charge the Confederate line." The hotel also served as one of the many field hospitals during the battles. In recent years, photos have begun to surface containing orbs and requests for investigations have been discussed.

Back in New Oxford, the New Oxford Cemetery has been the site of a P.E.E.R. investigation due, not only to intrigue, but also on the request of relatives who had reported seeing lights and orbs and hearing their deceased family members. This cemetery is where most of New Oxford's founding families have been buried, many of them who once lived in the Castles of New Oxford.

In the first chapter of this book, I posed a few questions. Now, nearing the end, I hope that I have provided a few answers. The first two questions I asked you were; did you ever wonder what it is that makes a place haunted and have you asked why there are ghosts or spirits here in this place? As described earlier in the book, a haunting can come in the form of a residual haunting like a tape player playing its imprinted image over and over again, or it can be an intelligent or interactive haunting where the disembodied spirit or soul of a person actually shares space with you and can even communicate with you. I believe that the common denominator here is that a haunting is the spirit activity of a once living human or animal. As to the question of why here, why in Adams County? Knowing the history of the area makes this question almost self-explanatory. So many people came together in one place in one short period of time, and that much concentrated energy and too much tragedy makes all this happen over and over. Just as we are drawn to Gettysburg and its surrounding communities to learn about the Civil War and attempt to understand how and why the battles happened here, so are the spirits who are still tied to these hallowed grounds.

To the next question, do ghosts really exist or is it just my imagination? Well, I think I've made my opinions quite clear in this matter. Imagination has nothing to do with it. Ghosts do exist. Just as you and I exist and walk this earth, so did and still do the spirits of the men and women who were here before us. The last question that I asked was; are we alone in this world? We never were alone and we probably never will be really alone. As I travel the country back roads of Adams County and walk the streets of downtown Gettysburg, I know that at times when I get a whiff of smoke, that my father is there with me and when a cold draft overtakes my body on a warm summer day or I feel a friendly nudge on the shoulder, I know that someone is tagging along, and I know that I'm not really alone. *My own personal experiences have taught me that I am usually walking along with Adams County Ghosts.*

Come to Adams County, visit Gettysburg, New Oxford, and the other small towns in South Central Pennsylvania, and I would bet that you too wouldn't be walking alone.

Bibliography

Ancestry.com online. *www.ancestry.com.*

Bates, Samuel P. *History of Cumberland and Adams Counties Pennsylvania.* Chicago, Illinois: Warner, Beers & Co., 1886.

Newspaper Archive online. *www.newspaperarchive.com.*

Adams County Historical Society, The. Gettysburg, Pennsylvania 17325.

Hunterstown Historical Society. *www.hunterstown1863. com.*

Index